MW00983383

SONGSCHOOL LATIN Book 1

Teacher's Edition

More *free* audio pronunciation aids are available on the *Song School Latin Book 1* product pages at ClassicalAcademicPress.com (click the Support tab beneath the product photo).

AMY REHN

Song School Latin Book 1 Teacher's Edition
© Classical Academic Press®, 2008
Version 1.3

All rights reserved. This publication may not be reproduced, stored in a
retrieval system, or transmitted, in any form or by any means,
without the prior written permission of Classical Academic Press.

Classical Academic Press
515 S. 32nd Street
Camp Hill, PA 17011

www.ClassicalAcademicPress.com

ISBN: 978-1-60051-046-5

Song School Latin Book 1 Music Credits:
Alec Nauck-Heisey: Guitarist & Vocals
Carolyn Baddorf: Violin & Vocals

Book cover and 3D illustrations by
Rob Baddorf

Book design and illustrations by
David Gustafson

Table of Contents
for Teacher's Edition

Song School Latin *student book with answers*

Table of Contents

CD Track Information

Classical

Track Number & Name	Chapter	Page	Time
1. Salve/Vale Song	1	5	1:26
2. Latin Alphabet Song	1	5	0:37
3. Vale Song	1	5	0:54
4. Nomen Song	2	8	1:35
5. Latin Vowel Song	2	8	0:43
6. Quid Agis Chant	3	11	0:31
7. Quid Agis Song	4	18	1:13
8. Family Song	5	20	1:25
9. Salve Song	6	23	0:36
10. Silly Sally Chant	7	26	1:02
11. Build a Casa	8	29	1:17
12. Classroom Commands Song	10	37	0:37
13. Classroom Commands Song (Cont.)	11	41	0:34
14. Manners Song	12	45	2:25
15. Animal Song	14	54	1:08
16. Animal Song (Cont.)	15	57	0:32
17. Christmas Chant	16	60	0:24
18. Christmas Chant (Cont.)	17	64	0:14
19. Action Song	19	73	1:13
20. Action Song (Cont.)	20	77	1:12
21. Edo Song	21	80	1:06
22. Cibus Chant	22	83	0:21
23. Canis Song	23	90	1:14
24. Weather Song	24	93	1:34
25. Seasons Song	25	96	0:47
26. Caelum Song	26	99	0:35
27. Row Your Navis	28	106	0:33
28. Hortus Song	29	109	1:00
29. Hiking Song	30	112	0:42
30. Sailing Song	31	118	1:10

Ecclesiastical

Track Number & Name	Chapter	Page	Time
31. Salve/Vale Song	1	5	1:27
32. Latin Alphabet Song	1	5	0:37
33. Vale Song	1	5	0:55
34. Nomen Song	2	8	1:35
35. Latin Vowel Song	2	8	0:43
36. Quid Agis Chant	3	11	0:31
37. Quid Agis Song	4	18	1:13
38. Family Song	5	20	1:25
39. Salve Song	6	23	0:36
40. Silly Sally Chant	7	26	1:02
41. Build a Casa	8	29	1:17
42. Classroom Commands Song	10	37	0:37
43. Classroom Commands Song (Cont.)	11	41	0:35
44. Manners Song	12	45	1:06
45. Animal Song	14	54	1:09
46. Animal Song (Cont.)	15	57	0:32
47. Christmas Chant	16	60	0:24
48. Christmas Chant (Cont.)	17	64	0:14
49. Action Song	19	73	1:13
50. Action Song (Cont.)	20	77	1:12
51. Edo Song	21	80	1:06
52. Cibus Chant	22	83	0:21
53. Canis Song	23	90	1:14
54. Weather Song	24	93	1:33
55. Seasons Song	25	96	0:47
56. Caelum Song	26	99	0:35
57. Row Your Navis	28	106	0:34
58. Hortus Song	29	109	1:00
59. Hiking Song	30	112	0:41
60. Sailing Song	31	118	1:10

Check out **Flash Dash**, our *free* online flash card game, to practice your vocabulary @ www.ClassicalAcademicPress.com

Classical Pronunciation

There are 24 letters in the Latin alphabet—there is no *j* or *w*. The letters *k, y* and *z* were used very rarely. Letters in Latin are never silent. There are two systems of pronunciation in Latin—classical and ecclesiastical.

Latin Consonants: Consonants are pronounced the same as in English with these exceptions.

Letter	Pronunciation	Example	Sound
b	before s or t like English **p**	**urbs:** city	*urps*
c / ch	always hard like English **k**	**cantō:** I sing	*kahn-toh*
g	always hard like English **g**oat	**gaudium:** joy	*gow-diyum*
gn	in the middle of the word like English **ngn** in ha**ngn**ail	**magnus:** big	*mang-nus*
i	before a vowel it is a consonant like the English **y**	**iaceō:** I lie down	*yah-keh-oh*
r	should be rolled as in Spanish or Italian	**rēgīna:** queen	*ray-geen-ah*
s	always like the **s** in the English sing	**servus:** servant	*ser-wus*
v	always as an English **w**	**vallum:** wall	*wa-luhm*

Diphthongs: Diphthongs are two vowels with a single sound.

ae	au	ei	oe	ui
as in **eye**	as in **out**	as in **stray**	as in **coil**	not a diphthong; pronounced **oo-ee**

Latin Short and Long Vowels: Vowels can be short or long in Latin. When they are long, they have a little dash called a macron placed over them. Long vowels take about twice as long to say as short ones. (We will not be using macrons in this book, but the audio CD will guide you so you pronounce vowels correctly.)

Short Vowels			Long Vowels		
LETTER	EXAMPLE	SOUND	LETTER	EXAMPLE	SOUND
a in Dinah	**casa:** house	*ka-sa*	**ā** in father	**stāre:** to stand	*stah-reh*
e in pet	**ventus:** wind	*wen-tus*	**ē** in they	**vidēre:** to see	*wi-dey-reh*
i in pit	**silva:** forest	*sil-wah*	**ī** in machine	**īre:** to go	*ee-reh*
o in pot	**bonus:** good	*bah-nus*	**ō** in hose	**errō:** I wander	*er-roh*
u in put	**cum:** with	*kum*	**ū** in rude	**lūdus:** school	*loo-duhs*

Classical or Ecclesiastical Pronunciation?

Both pronunciations are really quite similar, so ultimately the decision is not a significant one. The classical attempts to follow the way the Romans spoke Latin (an older pronunciation) while the ecclesiastical follows the way Latin pronunciation evolved within the Christian Church during the Middle Ages, particularly within the Roman Catholic Church.

The main difference between the two pronunciations is the way *c/ch* and *v* are pronounced. The classical pronounces *c/ch* as an English *k*, whereas the ecclesiastical pronounces it (Italian style) as an English *ch* (as in check). The ecclesiastical pronounces *v* as the English *v* (as in victory) whereas the classical pronounces it as an English *w*. In the ecclesiastical, a *j* occasionally appears in place of an *i* and the *t* has a special pronunciation, like *ts* as in cats.

So, take your pick and stick with it! Either choice is a good one. Our audio and video files contain both pronunciations.

Ecclesiastical Pronunciation

There is no *w* in the ecclesiastical pronunciation of Latin. The letters *k, y,* and *z* were used very rarely. Letters in Latin are never silent.

Latin Consonants: In the ecclesiastical pronunciation, consonants are pronounced the same as they are in English with the following exceptions. The pronunciations specific to the ecclesiastical pronunciation have been shaded.

Letter	Pronunciation	Example	Sound
b	before s or t like English **p**	**urbs:** city	*urps*
c	before e, i, ae, oe and y always like English **ch**	**cēna:** food	*chey-nah*
c	before other letters, hard c like English **c**ap	**cantō:** I sing	*kahn-toh*
g	soft before **e, i, ae, oe** like English **g**erm	**magistra:** teacher	*mah-jee-stra*
g	before other letters, hard like English **g**oat	**gaudium:** joy	*gow-diyum*
gn	in the middle of the word like English **ngn** in ha**ngn**ail	**magnus:** big	*mang-nus*
j	like the English **y** in yes	**jaceō:** I lie down	*yah-chey-oh*
r	should be rolled as in Spanish or Italian	**rēgīna:** queen	*ray-jeen-ah*
s	always like the s in the English sing	**servus:** servant	*ser-vus*
t	when followed by **i** and a vowel, like **tsee**	**silentium:** silence	*see-len-tsee-um*
v	always as an English **v**	**vallum:** wall	*va-luhm*

Diphthongs: With the exception of *ae*, which is pronounced "ay" in the ecclesiastical pronunciation, diphthongs are pronounced the same in both classical and ecclesiastical pronunciations. See the chart on the previous page for the other pronunciations.

Latin Short and Long Vowels: Vowels can be short or long in Latin. When they are long, they have a little dash called a macron placed over them. Long vowels take about twice as long to say as short ones. The ecclesiastical short and long vowels are pronounced in the same way as in the classical pronunciation. See the table on the preceding page.

Words to Learn

1. **salve** — hello
2. **vale** — good-bye
3. **discipuli** — students
4. **magister** — male teacher
   magistra — female teacher

Chapter Songs

<u>Salve/Vale Song</u> [Track 1(C)/31(E)]
Here comes **magistra**,
Salve, salve!
Teach the **discipuli**!
Students, students!
Away goes **magistra**,
Vale, vale!
Good-bye, **discipuli**!
Good-bye, students!

<u>Latin Alphabet Song</u> [Track 2(C)/32(E)]
A B C D E F G (clap), H I J* K L M N O P (clap),
Q R S T U and V (clap), X Y Z (clap-clap).

<u>Vale Song</u> [Track 3(C)/33(E)]
Vale! Vale!
Time to go, time to go, **vale**.
It's the end of the day,
And time to say,
Vale, vale, time to go.

*The J is not in the alphabet used with the classical pronunciation, but is in the alphabet used with the ecclesiastical pronunciation.

5

Chapter Lesson

* The Latin alphabet is just like our English alphabet except that it is missing one letter—**W**! This means it has twenty-five letters instead of the twenty-six we have. The letter **J** is used by those using the ecclesiastical pronunciation of Latin, but is not used by those using the classical pronunciation of Latin. Those using the classical pronunciation will just use an **I** in place of the **J**! You can hear how the Latin letters are pronounced by studying the pronunciation guide and by listening to your teacher or the audio CD included with this book.

Practice Your Latin

1. Practice writing **salve** and **vale** by tracing the dots.

   ~~Salve   Vale~~

2. Practice writing letters A through H by tracing the dots.

   ~~A B C D E F G H~~

3. Draw a picture of your **magistra** or **magister** in the box to the right.

4. Practice saying "hello" and "good-bye"
   to each other and to your teacher in Latin.

Grow Your English

The word "disciple" in English means "a follower." It was made out of a Latin word that you know! Which one of your new Latin words looks like the English word "disciple?" Circle one:

Vale   (Discipuli)   Magister   Salve

> **Teacher's Notes**
>
> *As anyone can see, the Roman alphabet has been adopted by the English alphabet. It is virtually the same, with the exception of a missing W. The original Roman alphabet had no J—this was added later and incorporated into the alphabet by the Roman Catholic Church. Thus, the "ecclesiastical" pronunciation of Latin includes a J that replaces I, usually at the beginning of words. It is pronounced just like the Roman I with a "y" sound.
>
> Teachers should choose either the classical or ecclesiastical style of pronunciation and spelling, while giving students an initial exposure to both. The differences are minimal (hinging mainly on the pronunciation of C and V and the addition of the letter J in the ecclesiastical system) and should not cause great frustration in students as long as the teacher chooses one system with which to teach. The companion audio CD features both systems of pronunciation—just choose "classical" or "ecclesiastical" when playing the CD. The text will include both spellings of a word that can begin with either an I (classical) or a J (ecclesiastical). Both a classical and an ecclesiastical pronunciation guide are included at the beginning of the book.

Chapter 1: Greeting Words

7

Chapter Story

Listen to your teacher read the story and fill in the blanks with either **salve** or **vale**.

This is Hare. ____Salve____, Hare! He is fast and likes to run races. One day he challenged big, slow

Tortoise to a race. This is Tortoise. ____Salve____, Tortoise! As they began, Hare ran far away into the

distance. ____Vale____, Hare! After running so hard, Hare got tired and took a nap. While he slept,

slow Tortoise caught up to him. ____Salve____ Tortoise! When Hare awoke, he ran after Tortoise, but it was too late. All

of the animals watched Tortoise come toward the finish line and shouted, "____Salve____, Tortoise!" Hare was very sad

that he lost and scurried down into his hole to hide. ____Vale____, Hare!

Show What You Know

1. How do you say "hello" in Latin? _____salve_____

2. How do you say "good-bye" in Latin? _____vale_____

3. What is the word for "teacher" in Latin? magister/magistra

4. What is the one letter English missing from the Latin alphabet? _____W_____

Chapter 2

Making Friends

Words to Learn

1. **Quid est tuum praenomen?**   What is your name?
2. **Meum praenomen est…**   My name is…

Chapter Songs

<u>Nomen Song</u> [Track 4(C)/34(E)]

Quid est tuum praenomen?
Quid est tuum praenomen?
Quid est tuum praenomen?
Tell me what your name is.

Meum praenomen est,
Meum praenomen est,
Meum praenomen est,
My name is _____.

QUID EST TUUM PRAENOMEN?

<u>Latin Vowels Song</u> [Track 5(C)/35(E)]

A says **ah** and sometimes **uh**.
E says **ay** and sometimes **eh**.
I says **ee** and also **ih**.
O says **oh** and sometimes **ah**.
U says **oo** and also **uh**.
This is our Latin vowel song.

Chapter Lesson

There are five vowels in the Latin alphabet, just as in the English alphabet. The letter **Y** is never counted as a vowel in Latin. The Latin vowels work in the same way that English vowels work, and they even look the same. They make different sounds, though. You will have to work hard to remember the sounds they make! The more you sing the vowels song and listen to the audio CD, the easier it will be. You can also chant through the sounds listed below to help you remember them.

A says **ah**, as in w<u>a</u>ter and also **uh** as in Di<u>n</u>ah.
E says **ay**, as in th<u>ey</u> and also **eh** as in p<u>e</u>t.
I says **ee**, as in mach<u>i</u>ne and also **ih** as in p<u>i</u>n.
O says **oh**, as in cl<u>o</u>ver and also **ah** as in p<u>o</u>t.
U says **oo**, as in r<u>u</u>de and also **uh** as in p<u>u</u>t.

Practice Your Latin

1. Practice writing your new words by tracing the dots.

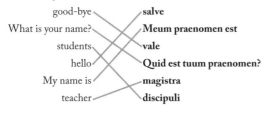

Quid est tuum praenomen?

Meum praenomen est

2. Practice writing the Latin alphabet I through Q by tracing the dots.

I J K L M N O P Q

3. Write the Latin vowels for each sound.

ay	ee	oo	oh	ah
E	I	U	O	A or O

---

4. Match the English words to the Latin words.

good-bye — **salve**
What is your name? — **Meum praenomen est**
students — **vale**
hello — **Quid est tuum praenomen?**
My name is — **magistra**
teacher — **discipuli**

5. Speaking Latin, ask three people what their names are.

Show What You Know

For questions 1 to 4 below, circle A or B.

1. How do you say "What is your name?" in Latin?

    (A. **Quid est tuum praenomen**)   B. **Meum praenomen est**

2. How do you say "My name is…" in Latin?

    A. **Quid est tuum praenomen**   (B. **Meum praenomen est**)

3. When you leave you say:

    A. **salve**   (B. **vale**)

4. When you come back you say:

    (A. **salve**)   B. **vale**

5. The Latin alphabet is missing which letter? _____ W _____

*6. Circle the correct Latin vowel for each sound.

    a. ee A (I)   b. oh (O) A   c. ah U (A)   d. ay (E) O

> **Teacher's Notes**
>
> *Say the sounds aloud for the students as they choose the answers. Have the students repeat the sound back to you.

Words to Learn

1. **Quid agis?** How are you?
2. **sum** I am
3. **bene** well/fine
4. **optime** great
5. **pessime** terrible

QUID AGIS?

Chapter Songs

* <u>Quid Agis Chant</u> [Track 6(C)/36(E)]

Hey, HEY! **Quid agis**?
Tell me how you are, friend.
Sum, sum! Sum bene!
I am doing fine, fine!

Hey, HEY! **Quid agis**?
Tell me how you are, friend.
Sum, sum! Optime!
I am doing great, great!

Hey, HEY! **Quid agis**?
Tell me how you are, friend.
Sum, sum! Pessime!
I am doing terrible!

> **Teacher's Notes**
> *Optional: Clap on the second and fourth beat.
> Split students into two groups and have them alternate the questions/responses.

11

Chapter Lesson

Did you notice that sometimes it takes fewer words to say something in Latin than in English? That is because of the special endings on many Latin words. These endings can mean "I" and "you" and many other things. The "s" at the end of the phrase **"Quid agis"** is the part that means "you." Endings on Latin words are like secret codes. You have to crack the code to find the word's real meaning.

Discipuli is a word that you learned in lesson one. I'm sure you remember that it means "students." What if you want to talk about only *one* student at a time, though? You have to change the sound at the end of the word. If you are talking about a girl student, the word is **discipula**. The vowel **a** sounds like *uh*. A boy student is a **discipulus**. Say the ending so that it rhymes with "fuss!" **Discipula** = girl student. **Discipulus** = boy student. Are you a **discipula** or a **discipulus**?

Grow Your English

An "optimist" is someone who always expects the best to happen. Circle the Latin word that sounds the most like "optimist."

Pessime **Salve** **Bene** (**Optime**)

Practice Your Latin

1. Practice writing vocabulary by tracing the dots.

Quid agis? Sum Bene
Optime Pessime

2. Practice writing the Latin alphabet R through Z by tracing the dots.

R S T U V X Y Z

3. Write the Latin word that describes how each person feels.

She looks like she feels _____optime_____.   She looks like she feels _____pessime_____.

4. Draw a picture of your face and complete the sentence.

Sum _____bene, optime, pessime_____

(Answers will vary.)

5. Ask three people how they are in Latin and then circle their responses.

Person 1:   **bene**   **optime**   **pessime**

Person 2:   **bene**   **optime**   **pessime**

Person 3:   **bene**   **optime**   **pessime**

6. Fill in the Latin word that fits best.

How do you feel when you get an ice cream cone? _____optime_____

How do you feel when you fall down and scrape your knee? _____pessime_____

How do you feel when you are well? _____bene_____

Show What You Know

For exercises 1 to 4, circle the correct English word or phrase.

1. **Quid agis** means: I am fine   (How are you?)   My name is

2. **Pessime** means: (terrible)   great   well/fine

3. **Bene** means: terrible   great   (well/fine)

4. **Optime** means: terrible   (great)   well/fine

5. What does **sum** mean? _____I am_____

Review

Circle the correct Latin word.

1. When you leave, you say: **salve** / (**vale**).

2. When you arrive, you say: (**salve**) / **vale**.

3. The person who teaches you is a: (**magister**) / **discipulus**.

Chapter 4

Master Your Words

Well, **discipuli**, you have learned about ten Latin words and three Latin phrases! Now it is time to take a week and make sure you have truly mastered your words. Can you give the correct English word for every Latin word below?

Chapter 1 Words

1. **salve** _____hello_____

2. **vale** _____good-bye_____

3. **discipuli** _____students_____

4. **magister** _____male teacher_____

5. **magistra** _____female teacher_____

Chapter 2 Phrases

1. **Quid est tuum praenomen?**   What is _____your name_____?

2. **Meum praenomen est…**   My _____name is_____ …

Chapter 3 Words/Phrases

1. **Quid agis?**   How _____are you_____?

2. **sum** _____I am_____

3. **bene** _____well/fine_____

4. **optime** _____great_____

5. **pessime** _____terrible_____

Master Your Songs

<u>Salve/Vale Song</u> [Track 1(C)/31(E)]

Here comes **magistra**,
Salve, salve!

Teach the **discipuli**!
Students, students!

Away goes **magistra**,
Vale, vale!

Good-bye, **discipuli**!
Good-bye, students!

<u>Latin Alphabet Song</u> [Track 2(C)/32(E)]

A B C D E F G (clap),
H I J K L M N O P (clap),
Q R S T U and V (clap),
X Y Z (clap-clap).

<u>Vale Song</u> [Track 3(C)/33(E)]

Vale! Vale!
Time to go, time to go, **vale**.
It's the end of the day,
And time to say,
Vale, vale, time to go.

<u>Nomen Song</u> [Track 4(C)/34(E)]

Quid est tuum praenomen?
Quid est tuum praenomen?
Quid est tuum praenomen?
Tell me what your name is.

Meum praenomen est,
Meum praenomen est,
Meum praenomen est,
My name is _____.

<u>Latin Vowels Song</u> [Track 5(C)/35(E)]

A says **ah** and sometimes **uh**.
E says **ay** and sometimes **eh**.
I says **ee** and also **ih**.
O says **oh** and sometimes **ah**.
U says **oo** and also **uh**.
This is our Latin vowel song.

<u>Quid Agis Chant</u> *(See if you remember all the verses.)* [Track 6(C)/36(E)]

Hey, HEY! **Quid agis?**
Tell me how you are, friend.
Sum, sum! Sum bene!
I am doing fine, fine!

<u>Quid Agis Song</u> [Track 7(C)/37(E)]

Quid agis means how are you?
How are you? How are you?
Quid agis means how are you?
Su-um bene.

(The CD contains additional verses with these final lines.)

Su-um tristis. ("I am sad.")

Su-um iratus. ("I am angry.")

Su-um optime. ("I am great.")

> **Teacher's Notes**
>
> Additional Activity: Provide cutouts or an outline of three children. Have students use pipe cleaners, clay, or some other material to make faces for the cutouts, with each one representing a different feeling: optime, pessime, or bene.

Activities

1. Match the Latin words to the English words.

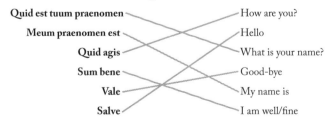

Latin	English
Quid est tuum praenomen	How are you?
Meum praenomen est	Hello
Quid agis	What is your name?
Sum bene	Good-bye
Vale	My name is
Salve	I am well/fine

2. Circle the Latin word that fits. (Answers will vary.)

   a. My teacher is a **discipulus /** (**magister**) (**magistra**) **/ vale**.

   b. My teacher teaches the **salve / magistra /** (**discipuli**).

   c. The (**discipuli**) **/ magister** should listen to the **discipuli /** (**magister**).

Chapter Story

<u>The Three Little Pigs</u>
*Listen for the Latin words and circle them as your **magistra** or **magister** reads the story.*

Once upon a time, there were three little pigs. When they grew up, they left home to build their own houses. **Valete*** little pigs! The first little pig met a man who was carrying a bundle of straw. "**Salve!**" said the little pig. "**Quid est tuum praenomen?**"

The man answered, "**Meum praenomen est** Bob."

The little pig said, "Would you please give me some straw to build a house?" So Bob gave him straw and the little pig started building his house. When he was finished, he heard a knock at the door. "**Quid est tuum praenomen?**" he asked.

"**Meum praenomen est** wolf," said the wolf. "**Quid agis?**"

"**Sum optime!**" said the little pig.

"May I come in?" asked the wolf. But the little pig knew the wolf was bad, so he said, "Not by the hair of my chinny-chin-chin!"

"Then I will huff and puff and blow your house in!" said the wolf. And he did.

The second little pig met a man who was carrying a load of sticks. "**Salve!**" he said. "**Quid agis?**"

"**Sum bene,**" the man replied.

"I would like to have some sticks to build a house," said the little pig. So the man gave him the sticks. When the little pig finished building the house, guess who knocked on his door? The big bad wolf!

"**Quid est tuum praenomen?**" asked the second little pig.

"**Meum praenomen est** wolf."

"You can't come in!" said the little pig. "Not by the hair of my chinny-chin-chin!" "Then I will huff and puff and blow your house in!" the wolf said. And he did!

The third little pig wanted a strong house. So, when he met a man who was carrying a load of bricks, he said "**Salve! Quid agis?**"

"**Sum pessime!**" said the man. "These bricks are too heavy for me! Would you like to have some of them?" So the third little pig built his house out of bricks.

Then the big bad wolf came along and knocked on his door. "Let me come in, little pig!" he said. "Not by the hair of my chinny-chin-chin!" said the little pig.

"Then I will huff and puff and blow your house in!" said the wolf. And he huffed and he puffed and he huffed and he puffed, but he could not blow that house in. He went away, and the little pig was safe in his house. **Vale**, wolf!

***Valete** is the way we say "good-bye" to two or more people.

Chapter 5   Family Members

Words to Learn

1. **pater**   father
2. **mater**   mother
3. **soror**   sister
4. **frater**   brother

Chapter Song

<u>Family Song</u> [Track 8(C)/38(E)]

My **pater** is really my father,
My **mater** is really my mom.
*My **frater** is my little brother,
And I am the **soror**, you see.

Pater, pater. Pater is really my father.
Mater, mater. Mater is really my mom.

(Repeat first verse.)

Frater, frater. Frater is my little brother.
I am the **soror**, and this is my family.

(*Repeat with: "My **soror** is my little sister, And I am the **frater**, you see.")

Chapter Lesson

The words in this chapter are very easy to learn. You can practice them every day when you talk to your family. Use the greetings that you have learned in Latin: **Salve, Mater!** or **Quid agis, Pater?** and **Vale, soror!** You can even greet a friend by name: "**Salve**, John! **Salve**, Susan!"

Practice Your Latin

1. Write the vocabulary words by tracing the dots.

<u>Pater Mater Soror Frater</u>

2. Match the pictures to their Latin names.

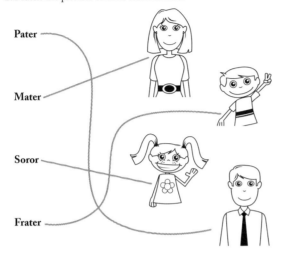

Pater

Mater

Soror

Frater

3. In the box to the right, draw a picture of your family doing something together and label each person with his or her Latin name.

Show What You Know

Circle the correct English word.

1. **frater**	(brother)	mother	sister
2. **soror**	brother	(sister)	father
3. **mater**	(mother)	father	sister
4. **pater**	mother	(father)	brother
5. **bene**	great	(well/fine)	father
6. **optime**	(great)	terrible	mother

Zzzzzzzzz

Words to Learn

1. **puella**   girl
2. **puer**   boy
3. **vir**   man
4. **femina**   woman

Chapter Song

<u>Salve Song</u> [Track 9(C)/39(E)]

When boys get up in the morning,
You say "**Salve, puer!**"
When girls get up in the morning,
Say "**Salve, puella!**"
(clap, clap)

Each boy grows into a man,
And then he is a **vir**.
Each girl grows into a woman,
She is a **femina**.
(clap, clap)

Chapter Lesson

Are you a **puer** or a **puella**? You know three words in Latin now that you can call yourself. You are a **puer** or **puella**, a **discipulus** or **discipula**, and you may be a **soror** or **frater**. The words in this chapter are a type called nouns. Nouns usually name a person, place, or thing. Can you think of any other Latin nouns that you have learned? How many nouns can you think of in English? There are too many to count!

23

Practice Your Latin

1. Write out the vocabulary words by tracing the dots.

Puella   Puer   Vir   Femina

2. Circle the correct Latin word.

My **pater** is a: puer   femina   (vir)

My **soror** is a: femina   vir   (puella)

My **frater** is a: vir   (puer)   puella

My **mater** is a: (femina)   puella   puer

3. Color and cut out the **vir**, **femina**, **puer** and **puella** and label with their Latin names. (See page 127 for larger cutouts.) Be ready to hold them up when the teacher calls the Latin words!

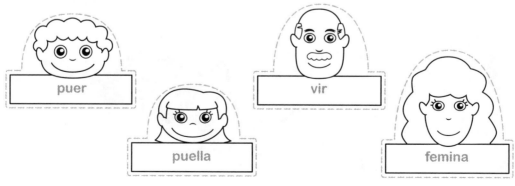

puer

puella

vir

femina

4. Draw lines to put the cookies in the right jar.

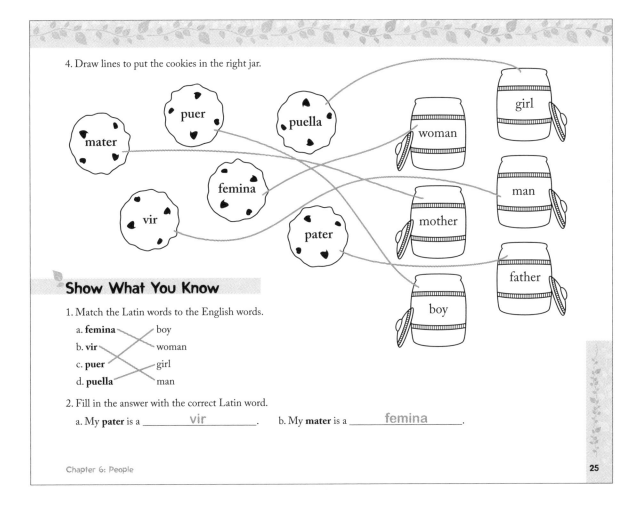

Show What You Know

1. Match the Latin words to the English words.

   a. **femina** — boy
   b. **vir** — woman
   c. **puer** — girl
   d. **puella** — man

2. Fill in the answer with the correct Latin word.

   a. My **pater** is a _____ vir _____.   b. My **mater** is a _____ femina _____.

Chapter 7   Classroom Items

Words to Learn

1. **mensa**   table
2. **sella**   chair
3. **stylus**   pencil
4. **liber**   book

Chapter Song

<u>Silly Sally Chant</u> [Track 10(C)/40(E)]

Silly Sally sat in her **sella**,
Eating her curds and whey,
Along came Miss Molly and sat on the **mensa**,
But her **mater** chased her away.

Serious Sam picked up a **stylus**,
And started to write in a book,
Till Luke came along and looked at that **liber**,
And said "That's MY book you took!"

Teacher's Notes
For the chant, have the children clap to the beat!

Chapter Lesson

Do you remember what we called the type of words in the last chapter? Do you think these new words are of the same type? Remember that nouns usually name a person, place, or thing. If you can touch it, you know it's a noun! Some nouns are things that you can't touch, though, like "song." Practice saying your new words aloud while touching each item that they name. You can call your desk a **mensa**.

Practice Your Latin

1. Practice writing your new words by tracing the dots.

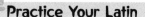

Mensa Sella Stylus Liber

2. Color and cut out the pictures of these objects and label them in Latin (see page 129 for larger cutouts).

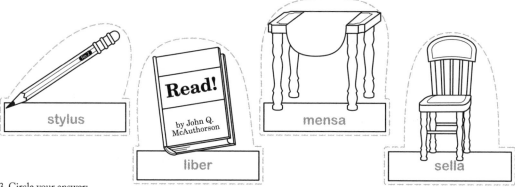

stylus

Read! by John Q. McAuthorson

liber

mensa

sella

3. Circle your answer:

Should you sit on a **mensa** or a **sella**?	(sella)	mensa
Do you write with a **stylus** or a **sella**?	sella	(stylus)
Do you put your food on the **mensa** or on the **liber**?	liber	(mensa)
Do you read a **liber** or a **stylus**?	(liber)	stylus

Chapter 7: Classroom Items

27

Grow Your English

"Library" is an English word that was made out of one of these Latin words. Think about what you find in a library. Which Latin word do you think "library" came from? Circle your answer.

mensa   stylus   (liber)   sella

Show What You Know

For questions 1 to 4, circle the correct English word:

1. **stylus**   (pencil)   table   chair

2. **sella**   table   (chair)   book

3. **mensa**   book   chair   (table)

4. **liber**   chair   (book)   pencil

For questions 5 to 6, circle the correct Latin word:

5. What Latin word did "library" come from?   sella   mensa   (liber)

6. Tell me how you are in Latin: **Sum optime / pessime / bene.**
   (Answers will vary.)

28

Chapter 7: Classroom Items

Song School Latin Teacher's Edition

18

Household Items **Chapter 8**

Words to Learn

1. **casa**   house
2. **porta**   door
3. **murus**   wall
4. **fenestra**   window

Chapter Song

<u>Build a Casa</u> [Track 11(C)/41(E)]

Build a **casa**, build a **casa**,
Make it nice and tall.
Don't forget to paint the **murus**,
Paint the pretty wall.
Make a window, a **fenestra**,
Let in all the light.
And make a door, a great big **porta**,
Shut it tight at night.

Chapter Lesson

Can you touch all of the things named by our new Latin words? If so, what do you call this type of word? Latin nouns are grouped into five families. These families are called *declensions*. The Latin nouns that end with the letter "a" are in the first family, or the *first declension*. Can you pick out which of your new words are in the first declension?

29

Practice Your Latin

1. Practice writing your new words by tracing the dots.

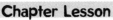
Casa Porta Murus Fenestra

2. Draw a **casa** on a blank sheet of paper. Label the door, windows and walls with the Latin words.

* 3. Build a **casa** with craft materials. Put Latin labels on the parts.

4. Choose the Latin word that fits best.

It's raining! Let's go into the _____casa_____ (**casa/murus**).

There is a bird chirping! Look out the _____fenestra_____ (**fenestra/murus**) to find it.

It's cold outside! Shut the _____porta_____ (**murus/porta**).

I hung a painting on the _____murus_____ (**murus/casa**).

Grow Your English

A castle is a huge, fancy house for a king. It came from one of the Latin words in this chapter. Say "castle" out loud. Circle the Latin word that it makes you think of.

fenestra   murus   (casa)   porta

> **Teacher's Notes**
>
> *This exercise is optional if time or materials are short. It is a fun class project, though, if you can fit it in!
>
> Additional Activity: Label items in your school room with their Latin names and refer to them in Latin as much as possible. Use the vocabulary from lessons 7 and 8. If possible, have the students also make labels for items in their own homes.

30

Chapter 8: Household Items

Song School Latin Teacher's Edition   **19**

Show What You Know

Match the pictures to the Latin words.

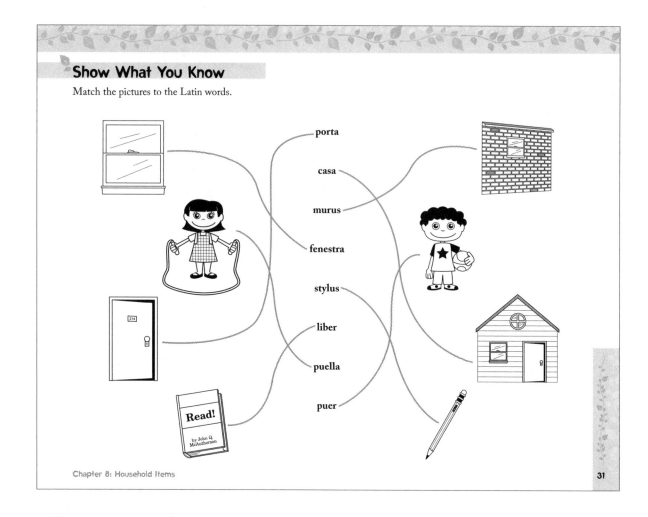

porta

casa

murus

fenestra

stylus

liber

puella

puer

Chapter 9   Review

Master Your Words

Well, **discipuli**, you have learned another 16 Latin words! Now it is time once again to make sure you have mastered all 16 of your words. Can you give the correct English word for every Latin word below?

Chapter 5 Words

1. **pater** _____father_____

2. **mater** _____mother_____

3. **soror** _____sister_____

4. **frater** _____brother_____

Chapter 6 Words

1. **puella** _____girl_____

2. **puer** _____boy_____

3. **vir** _____man_____

4. **femina** _____woman_____

Chapter 7 Words

1. **mensa**   table
2. **sella**   chair
3. **stylus**   pencil
4. **liber**   book

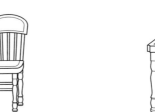
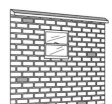

Chapter 8 Words

1. **casa**   house
2. **porta**   door
3. **murus**   wall
4. **fenestra**   window

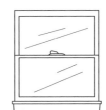

Master Your Songs

Family Song [Track 8(C)/38(E)]

My **pater** is really my father, My **mater** is really my mom.
My **frater** is my little brother, And I am the **soror**, you see.

Pater, **pater**. **Pater** is really my father. **Mater**, **mater**. **Mater** is really my mom.

(Repeat first verse.)

Frater, **frater**. **Frater** is my little brother. I am the **soror**, and this is my family.

(*Repeat with: "My **soror** is my little sister, And I am the **frater**, you see.")

Salve Song [Track 9(C)/39(E)]

When boys get up in the morning,
You say "**Salve**, **puer**!"
When girls get up in the morning,
Say "**Salve**, **puella**!"
(clap, clap)

Each boy grows into a man,
And then he is a **vir**.
Each girl grows into a woman,
She is a **femina**.
(clap, clap)

Read!
by John Q. McAuthorson

Silly Sally Chant [Track 10(C)/40(E)]

Silly Sally sat in her **sella**,
Eating her curds and whey,
Along came Miss Molly and sat on the **mensa**,
But her **mater** chased her away.

Serious Sam picked up a **stylus**,
And started to write in a book,
Till Luke came along and looked at that **liber**,
And said "That's MY book you took!"

Build a Casa [Track 11(C)/41(E)]

Build a **casa**, build a **casa**,
Make it nice and tall.
And don't forget to paint the **murus**,
Paint the pretty wall.

Make a window, a **fenestra**,
To let in all the light.
And make a door, a great big **porta**,
To shut up tight at night.

Activities

1. Match the Latin words to the correct pictures.

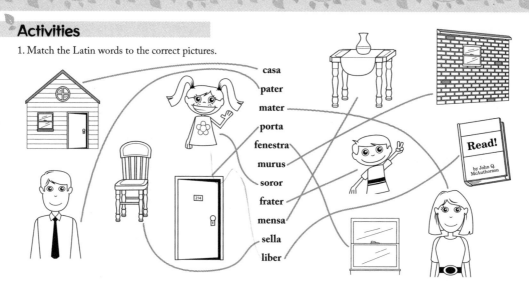

casa
pater
mater
porta
fenestra
murus
soror
frater
mensa
sella
liber

Chapter Story

Goldilocks and the Three Bears

Once upon a time, there was a **vir** and a **femina** who had a little **puella** named Goldilocks. She often worried them by wandering too far in the woods by herself. One day on a long walk she found a small **casa**. She went to the **fenestra** and peeked inside, but no one was there, so the little **puella** opened the **porta**, and went right in.

There was a **mensa** in the room, and sitting on it there were three full bowls of porridge. Goldilocks was hungry from her walk so she picked up the spoon of the first **crater** (bowl) of porridge and tasted it. "Ouch! It is too hot," she said. Then she tried the next **crater** on the **mensa**. "Yuck! It is too cold." So the little **puella** tried the last **crater**, and it was just right. "Yum."

After Goldilocks ate she was tired, so she walked through the **porta** to the living room to sit down. There were three chairs in the room, lined up along the **murus**. She went to the first **sella** and tried to climb up into it. "Err! This **sella** is too tall." So Goldilocks tried the second **sella**. "Ugh! This **sella** is too wide." Then she tried sitting in the last **sella**, and it was just right, but as she sat down it broke into pieces!

Goldilocks was upset and very sleepy now so she went upstairs to the bedroom to take a nap. There were three beds against the **murus** of the bedroom. She lay down in the first bed. "Oof! This **lectus** (bed) is too hard," she said. So she tried the next. "Oh! This lectus is too soft." So Goldilocks went to the last little **lectus** and lay down. It was just right and she took a nap.

While she slept, the owners of the **casa**, three bears, came home. The **Pater** bear was hungry and sat down at the **mensa** to eat. "Someone has been eating my porridge!" he yelled.

"Well, my, my, someone has been eating my porridge too!" said **Mater** bear.

"Well, someone ate all of my porridge!" cried the young **puer** bear. "My **crater** is empty!" So **Pater** and **Mater** bear shared their porridge with the **puer** bear, and they went through the **porta** to the living room to sit down. **Pater** bear growled and said, "Someone has been sitting in my **sella**!"

"Oh, honey," replied **Mater** bear, "Someone has been sitting in my **sella**, too!"

Then the poor **puer** bear shouted, "Someone sat in my **sella** and they broke it into pieces!"

So they went upstairs to rest in their beds, and **Pater** bear looked at his messy **lectus** and said, "Someone has been sleeping in my **lectus**!"

Mater bear gasped, "My heavens, someone has been sleeping in my **lectus**, too!"

But **Frater** bear yelled the loudest. "There is someone sleeping in my **lectus** right now!"

The little **puella** was terrified when she heard the yells and woke to find three big bears looking down at her, but **Mater** bear was kind and greeted her. "**Salve, puella. Quid agis?**"

"**Sum bene,**" Goldilocks answered very quietly.

Pater bear said, "You need to go home to your own **pater** and **mater** now, the poor **vir** and **femina** must be very worried. You may come back again and play with **puer** bear, as long as you promise not to break another **sella**."

"Yes sir," the little **puella** squeaked. She went home but often made visits, with her **pater** and **mater**'s permission, to the little **casa** in the woods.

Classroom Commands | Chapter 10

Words to Learn

1. **sede** — sit
   sedete — sit (to more than one person)
2. **surge** — rise/stand up
   surgite — rise/stand up (to more than one person)
3. **scribe** — write
   scribite — write (to more than one)
4. **repete** — repeat
   repetite — repeat (to more than one)

Chapter Song

Classroom Commands Song [Track 12(C)/42(E)]

Sede, sedete in your seat,
In your seat, in your seat.
Surge, surgite on your feet,
Stand up on your feet.

Scribe, scribite write so neat,
Write so neat, write so neat.
Repete, repitite,
After me repeat.

> **Teacher's Notes**
> Use actions or hand motions when practicing the vocabulary and singing the song.

sede = sit
surge = rise/stand up
scribe = write
repete = repeat

37

Chapter Lesson

* Did you notice that your new words in this chapter are all commands? These words are *not* nouns. Your **magistra** or **magister** will give you instructions in Latin now. Be sure to learn these words well so you will know what to do when that happens! Listen carefully to the endings on the commands. If there is a "te" sound on the end, the command is to more than one person. If there is no "te" on the end, the command is for only one. The first form of the word in the list is the command to one person. Practice saying the words both ways. Remember to listen carefully to the ending when your teacher gives a command!

Grow Your English

"Scribble" comes from a Latin word. Think about what it means and say it aloud. Which one of your new Latin words does it remind you of?

_____scribe_____

> **Teacher's Notes**
> *Stand in front of your students and give plural-form commands. Point to one student and give singular commands. Give commands faster and faster!
>
> There are four families of verbs, called conjugations. They all function in the same way; the key difference among them is the vowels that are on the end of the verb stems. Commands are formed in Latin by taking the "re" off of the infinitive form of the verb, leaving the verb stem. When a command is made plural, "te" is simply added to that stem. When a verb stem ends in a short "e," it changes to an "i" when the "te" is added to make it plural. Students do not need to understand any of this as they go through this book.

Practice Your Latin

1. Practice writing your new words by tracing the dots.

Sede Surge Scribe Repete
Sedete Surgite Scribite Repetite

38

Chapter 10: Classroom Commands

Song School Latin Teacher's Edition 23

2. Match the Latin commands to the thing that you would use to obey each one.

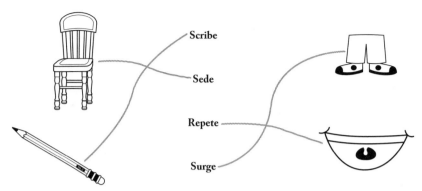

Scribe

Sede

Repete

Surge

* 3. Practice time! Listen carefully and follow the commands that your teacher gives you in Latin.

** 4. Practice using the commands on three other people. Be sure to follow commands that others give you!

5. Are these commands to one person, or more than one? Circle your answer.

a. **sedete**   one   (more than one)

b. **surge**   (one)   more than one

c. **scribe**   (one)   more than one

d. **repetite**   one   (more than one)

e. **sede**   (one)   more than one

Teacher's Notes

*Repeat four vocabulary words to students.

**Allow children to practice together, or give commands back to you.

Show What You Know

1. What commands are these children obeying? Circle your answer.

a.   (sede)   repetite   surge

b.   repetite   (scribe)   sede

c.   scribe   (surge)   sede

d.   surge   scribe   (repete)

2. What Latin word does "scribble" come from? _____ scribe _____

Song School Latin Teacher's Edition

24

More Classroom Commands — Chapter 11

Words to Learn

1. **audi**   listen
   audite   listen (to more than one person)
2. **tace**   be quiet
   tacete   be quiet (to more than one person)
3. **aperi librum**   open the book
   aperite libros   open the books (to more than one person)
* 4. **attole manum**   raise your hand
   attolite manus   raise your hands (to more than one person)

Chapter Song

<u>Classroom Commands Song (Continued)</u>
[Track 13(C)/43(E)]

Tace, tacete - quiet please,
Quiet please, quiet please.
Audi, audite listen up,
Listen up to me.

Aperi librum – open the book,
Open the book, open the book.
Attole manum – raise your hand,
Raise it nice and high.

> **Teacher's Notes**
> *Note that in this case "manum" and "manus" are actually the accusative forms of "manus, -us," a fourth declension noun. This should not be confused with "manus" as shown in chapter 19.

Chapter Lesson

* This chapter has four more commands for you to learn! Do you remember how to tell if a command is given to more than one person? What sound do we put on the end of a command if it is for more than one person? "Te," of course! When a command is to only one person, you say that it is singular. Think of the word "single." It means "only one." If a command is to more than one person, you say that it is plural. So, **audi** is a singular command. **Tacete** is a plural command. See the "te" on the end of **tacete**? You have to listen a little harder to the commands that have two words in them. The "te" is on the end of the first word of the command. **Attole manum** is a singular command, and **attolite manus** is a plural command. What about **sedete** and **scribite**? Are they singular or plural?

Practice Your Latin

1. Practice writing your new words by tracing the dots.

Audi Audite Tace
Aperi librum Aperit
Attole manum Attol

** 2. Practice a few commands that your teacher will speak to you.

3. Circle the command that you think the teacher should give.

   a. The students are not paying attention.   Attole manum!   (Audite!)

   b. The students are talking out of turn.   (Tacete!)   Aperite libros!

   c. The students need to practice writing their new words.   Audite!   (Aperite libros!)

> **Teacher's Notes**
> *You probably noticed that the endings on librum and manum changed along with the ending on the imperative verbs. The students are learning the correct form that these nouns should have when they are plural direct objects. If they are curious, just tell them that manum means hand and manus means hand and that sometimes their endings will vary (from -um to -us). You may tell them that later they will learn more about why the endings change, but that they do not need to be concerned about these variable endings at this point.
>
> **Use vocabulary from chapters 10 and 11.

4. Color the pictures. What commands are these children following? Match the pictures to the commands.

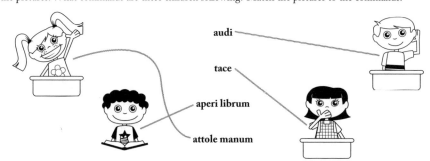

audi

tace

aperi librum

attole manum

5. Are these commands singular or plural? Circle the correct answer.

a. **sede** (singular) plural

b. **attolite manus** singular (plural)

c. **tacete** singular (plural)

d. **scribe** (singular) plural

e. **aperite libros** singular (plural)

f. **audite** singular (plural)

Grow Your English

The Latin word **audi** is the root of several words that you know in English. The word "audio" is talking about sound. You have probably heard it before. An "audience" is a group of people who are listening to some kind of sound. And the "auditorium" is the large room where you might see a concert or listen to a speaker. Latin is everywhere!

Show What You Know

Match the Latin words to the English words.

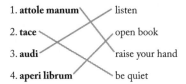

1. **attole manum**   listen

2. **tace**   open book

3. **audi**   raise your hand

4. **aperi librum**   be quiet

Review words

Circle the matching English word.

1. **sede**   stand   (sit)

2. **scribe**   (write)   stand

Are these commands to one person or to everyone? Circle the correct answer.

3. **tacite**   one person   (everyone)

4. **surge**   (one person)   everyone

5. **audi**   (one person)   everyone

6. **sedete**   one person   (everyone)

Write your answer.

7. What Latin word does "audience" come from? _____audi_____

Manners **Chapter 12**

Words to Learn

1. **amabo te** please
2. **tibi gratias ago** thank you
3. **ignosce mihi** excuse me

Chapter Song

<u>Manners Song</u> [Track 14(C)/44(E)]

When you ask for anything you have to say **amabo te**,
When you ask for anything you have to say **amabo te**.
If you really want to have it, don't just take it away,
Just say **amabo te**.

Tibi gratias ago means thank you very much,
Tibi gratias ago means thank you, thank you very much.
If your mom gives you a cookie, say before you eat it up,
Say **tibi gratias ago**.

Please excuse me is **ignosce mihi**, please excu-use me,
Please excuse me is **ignosce mihi**, please excu-use me.
If you bump into a little man and make him spill his tea,
Say **ignosce mihi**!

45

Practice Your Latin

1. Practice writing the phrases by tracing the dots.

Amabo te Tibi gratias ago
Ignosce mihi

2. Color the pictures and match them to the Latin phrases that you should use for situations pictured below.

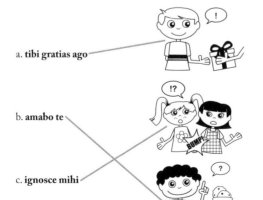

a. **tibi gratias ago**

b. **amabo te**

c. **ignosce mihi**

3. In the box to the right, draw a picture of something for which you said "**tibi gratias ago** (thank you)," today.

"**Tibi gratias ago**."

46

Chapter 12: Manners

Song School Latin Teacher's Edition 27

Show What You Know

Circle the correct English meaning for these Latin phrases.

1. **ignosce mihi**   please   thank you   (excuse me)

2. **amabo te**   (please)   thank you   excuse me

3. **tibi gratias ago**   please   (thank you)   excuse me

Review

Circle the correct English meaning for these Latin words.

1. **mensa**   (table)   chair   book

2. **mater**   brother   father   (mother)

3. **sedete**   listen   (sit)   stand

> **Teacher's Notes**
>
> Additional Activity: Have each child (or as many as time permits) take turns passing out something to the class, practicing "please" and "thank you."

Chapter 13   Review

Master Your Words

Well, **discipuli**, you have learned eight commands and three new Latin phrases! It is time once again to make sure you have mastered all of these new Latin words. Can you give the correct English word for every Latin word below?

Chapter 10 Words

1. **sede**   _sit_

    sedete   _sit (pl.)_

2. **surge**   _rise/stand up_

    surgite   _rise/stand up (pl.)_

3. **scribe**   _write_

    scribite   _write (pl.)_

4. **repete**   _repeat_

    repetite   _repeat (pl.)_

Chapter 11 Words/Phrases

1. **audi** _____ listen
   audite _____ listen (pl.)
2. **tace** _____ be quiet
   tacete _____ be quiet (pl.)
3. **aperi librum** _____ open the book
   aperite libros _____ open the book (pl.)
4. **attole manum** _____ raise your hand
   attolite manus _____ raise your hand (pl.)

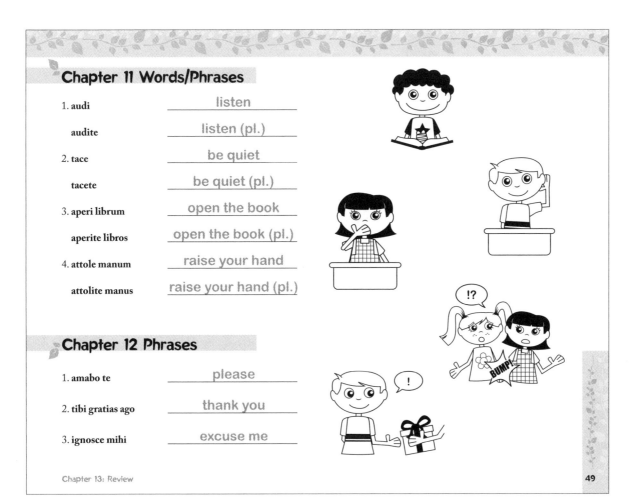

Chapter 12 Phrases

1. **amabo te** _____ please
2. **tibi gratias ago** _____ thank you
3. **ignosce mihi** _____ excuse me

Master Your Songs

<u>Classroom Commands Song</u> [Tracks 12-13(C)/42-43(E)]

Sede, **sedete** in your seat,
In your seat, in your seat.
Surge, **surgite** on your feet,
Stand up on your feet.

Scribe, **scribite** write so neat,
Write so neat, write so neat.
Repete, **repitite**
After me, repeat.

Tace, **tacete** – quiet please,
Quiet please, quiet please.
Audi, **audite** listen up,
Listen up to me.

Aperi librum – open the book,
Open the book, open the book.
Attole manum – raise your hand,
Raise it nice and high.

<u>Manners Song</u> [Track 14(C)/44(E)]

When you ask for anything you have to say **amabo te**,
When you ask for anything you have to say **amabo te**.
If you really want to have it, don't just take it away,
Just say **amabo te**.

Tibi gratias ago means thank you very much,
Tibi gratias ago means thank you, thank you very much.
If your mom gives you a cookie, say before you eat it up,
Say **tibi gratias ago**.

Please excuse me is **ignosce mihi**, please excu-use me,
Please excuse me is **ignosce mihi**, please excu-use me.
If you bump into a little man and make him spill his tea,
Say **ignosce mihi**!

Activities

1. What did the **magister** tell the **discipuli** to do? Circle the correct answer.

a. **attolite manus** / (aperite libros) / audite

b. sedete / (surgite) / tacete

c. (attolite manus) / amabo te / surgite

d. (sedete) / audite / ignosce mihi

e. surge / (tace) / vale

f. amabo te / tace / (audi)

g. sede / (scribe) / surge

---

2. What should these children say? Circle the correct answer:

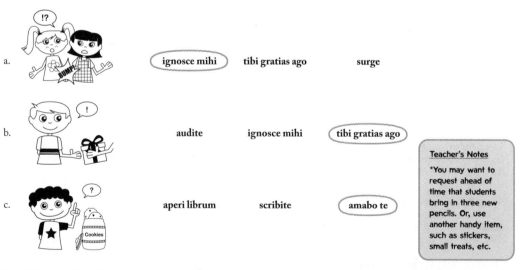

a.   (ignosce mihi)   tibi gratias ago   surge

b.   audite   ignosce mihi   (tibi gratias ago)

c.   aperi librum   scribite   (amabo te)

Teacher's Notes
*You may want to request ahead of time that students bring in three new pencils. Or, use another handy item, such as stickers, small treats, etc.

3. Play Simon Says! Listen as your teacher or a fellow student plays Simon and gives you commands. Remember you only have to obey when the leader first says, "Simon says…"

* 4. Have a pencil exchange! You will be giving pencils to three different people in your class. Here are the rules:

a. Greet each student in Latin.

b. Ask how they are in Latin.

c. Say **amabo te** for "please" when you request a pencil and **tibi gratias ago** for "thank you" when you are given a pencil.

Chapter Story

The Parable of the Vineyard

There was once a **vir**. Perhaps he was a **pater**. We do not know for sure. He had a large vineyard where grapes were grown. There were so many grapes in his vineyard that he needed help picking them, so early in the morning he went out to find some help. The first person he saw was a **puer**. "I see a **puer** to help me!" he shouted. He went quickly to the boy. "**Salve!**" he said. "**Quid agis?**"

The **puer** answered, "**Sum bene.**"

The **vir** said, "**Surge** and come help me in my vineyard, **amabo te**! I will pay you well."

"I will," agreed the **puer**. "I have a **mater** and **frater** and **soror**, and I must provide money for them so that they may buy food. I will be happy to work for you."

And so the **puer** began to work hard picking grapes in the vineyard.

The owner of the vineyard, however, soon realized that he would need more help, so he went out again and looked until he saw a **vir** writing in a **liber** with his **stylus**. "**Salve!**" called the owner. "**Quid agis?**"

"**Sum pessime**," said the **vir**. "I need money badly!"

"Then you are just the one I am looking for," said the owner. "Do not **sede**. Do not **scribe**. **Surge** and come! I need help picking grapes. I will pay you well."

"**Optime**," said the **vir**. "I will be glad to work for you!"

And so the two of them worked and worked, but still there were grapes left on the vines.

Finally, the owner of the vineyard found one last **vir** who might help him. He was a lazy fellow. The owner tripped over him because he was lying down! "**Ignosce mihi!**" said the owner. "**Audi** me! I need help in my vineyard. I will pay you well. **Surge!**" The **vir** was lazy, but the owner of the vineyard was offering him a lot of money for only a little work, so he agreed.

The day was finally done, and all the grapes had been picked from the vines. One by one the workers came to the owner to receive their wages. He paid each one the same amount, no matter how long he had worked. The last man went away happy with his money, shouting "**Valete!**" over his shoulder as he went. The others, however, were not happy. The **puer** who had worked since the morning thought he deserved more money because he had worked longer than those who had come in the afternoon and night time. The **puer** and the **vir** with the **liber** complained, but the owner just said, "It is my money. You agreed to these wages, and I have the right to be generous with my money if I like. **Valete!**"

—*Adapted from Matthew 20: 1-16*

Chapter 14   Pets

Words to Learn

1. **canis**   dog
2. **feles**   cat
3. **equus**   horse
4. **piscis**   fish

Chapter Song

Animal Song [Track 15(C)/45(E)]

Listen to the **canis** early in the morning,
Barking at the **feles** and makin' her run away.
"Meow" said the **feles** and went to catch a **piscis**,
And she climbed on an **equus** munching on his hay.
Neigh, neigh! Meow, meow! Off we go!

Chapter Lesson

Do you have any pets? If you do, you will probably learn its Latin name this week! Your new words are all animal names, and next week you will learn four more. Are animals things you can touch? Of course—just be careful about which ones you touch! That means these new Latin words are nouns. Do you remember that every Latin noun belongs to a family? There are five of these families, and they are called declensions. So, practice the animal words, and you can call everyone in your family by their Latin names, even your pets. Just don't call your dog a declension!

APPORTA!*

Teacher's Notes

Additional Activity: Have students bring in pictures of their pets and post them on the bulletin board with their Latin names.

*Apporta = Fetch

Practice Your Latin

1. Practice writing your new words by tracing the dots.

Canis   Feles   Equus   Piscis

2. Draw lines from the pictures to their Latin names.

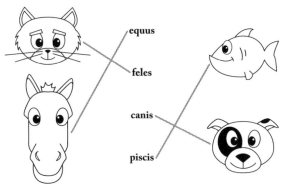

equus

feles

canis

piscis

3. Fill in the blanks with the Latin word that fits best.

a. The **puer** threw a stick for his _____canis_____ to fetch.

b. The **puella** put a saddle on her _____equus_____ and rode him away.

c. The **vir** went to the pond with his fishing rod to catch a _____piscis_____.

d. The _____feles_____ caught a big, fat mouse.

Show What You Know

Circle the correct English meaning for these Latin words.

1. **feles**	horse	fish	(cat)
2. **piscis**	dog	(fish)	horse
3. **canis**	(dog)	cat	fish
4. **equus**	fish	cat	(horse)

Review Words

Circle the correct English meaning for these Latin words.

1. **puella**	(girl)	boy	woman
2. **puer**	woman	girl	(boy)
3. **vir**	boy	(man)	woman
4. **femina**	man	girl	(woman)

Animals — Chapter 15

Words to Learn

1. **leo**   lion
2. **avis**   bird
3. **ursa**   bear
4. **elephantus**   elephant

Chapter Song

* <u>Animal Song (Continued)</u> [Track 16(C)/46(E)]

See the little **avis** flying 'round the **leo**,
"Roar" says the **leo** and scares away the bird.
Along comes the **ursa** and eats up all the honey,
Elephantus stomps around his little elephant herd.
Tweet, tweet! Roar, roar! Off we go!

Chapter Lesson

Last week you learned the word for dog—**canis**. Do you know that the Romans (who spoke Latin) used to warn people of mean dogs with signs just like we do? The way they said this in Latin was **cave canem** (beware of the dog!).

> **Teacher's Notes**
>
> *Practice this song as a continuation of the chapter 14 song. You might let individual students or rows of students take one line in turn—have one row or student be the bird, one the lion, etc. Encourage motions as you sing and practice the words. Each of the animals should have a representative motion or hand sign.

57

<u>Famous Latin Saying</u>

Each week from now on we will learn a famous Latin saying. Most of the sayings that you will learn are used by people who speak English. These Latin sayings are so famous that even people who speak English may know them!

This week work on memorizing **cave canem**—beware of the dog!

Practice Your Latin

1. Practice writing your new words by tracing the dots.

Leo   Avis   Ursa   Elephantus

2. Draw pictures of a lion, bird, bear, and elephant above their Latin names.

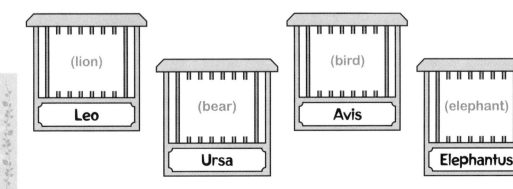

(lion) — **Leo**

(bear) — **Ursa**

(bird) — **Avis**

(elephant) — **Elephantus**

3. Match the Latin words to the English words.

a. **leo** ————————— lion

b. **avis** elephant

c. **ursa** bird

d. **elephantus** bear

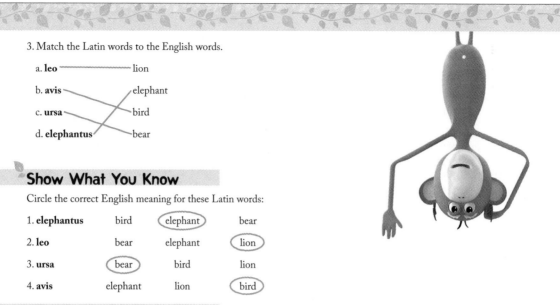

Show What You Know

Circle the correct English meaning for these Latin words:

1. **elephantus**   bird   (elephant)   bear
2. **leo**   bear   elephant   (lion)
3. **ursa**   (bear)   bird   lion
4. **avis**   elephant   lion   (bird)

Review Words

Circle the correct English meaning for these Latin words:

1. **feles**   dog   bird   (cat)
2. **equus**   (horse)   fish   cat
3. **discipuli**   teacher   (students)   horse
4. **puer**   (boy)   cat   girl

Chapter 16   Christmas Words

Words to Learn

1. **angelus**   angel
2. **pastor**   shepherd
3. **agnus**   lamb
4. **stella**   star
5. **infans**   baby

Chapter Song

<u>Christmas Chant</u> [Track 17(C)/47(E)]

Angelus – angel,
Stella – star,
Both appeared in the sky afar.

Pastor – shepherd,
Agnus – lamb,
Shepherds watching the little lambs.

Infans – baby,
Born in the hay,
Jesus, born on Christmas day.

LAETISSIMUS, ACCIPIAT, IAM MUNDUS DOMINUM.

Chapter Lesson

Christmas is coming soon and your new Latin words will help you remember the Christmas story. You also get to add one more animal name to your list—**agnus**! Did you notice that **stella** ends with an *a*? That means that it belongs to the first family of nouns, the first declension. **Infans** is another word that you can use all year. Is there an **infans** in your family? Have you ever had an **infans feles**?

Famous Latin Saying

This week your famous Latin saying is **rara avis**—"a rare bird." This phrase is not only used to describe a real **avis**, but also anything or anyone that is rare, unusual or interesting. You might call a friend who can throw a ball well with either hand a **rara avis**!

Grow Your English

Infans looks almost exactly like the English word "infant." That's because we borrowed it from Latin! It means the same thing in English as it does in Latin: a small baby.

Here is another English word that came from Latin: constellation. Constellation means a grouping of stars that make a shape in the sky. Have you ever seen the Big Dipper? That is part of a constellation known as Ursa Major. There are 88 known constellations, and they all have Latin names! Constellation is a long word, so the Latin is hard to find. If you look right in the middle of the word, though, you will see one of your new Latin words spelled out perfectly!

Practice Your Latin

1. Practice writing your new words by tracing the dots.

Angelus   Pastor   Agnus

Stella   Infans

2. Draw a line from the Latin words to the items in the picture.

angelus

pastor

stella

agnus

3. Fill in the sentences with the Latin word that fits best.

a. The ____pastor____ was out in the field watching his flock.

b. The ____stella____ led the wise men to Bethlehem.

c. We were all born as a little ____infans____.

d. The ____angelus____ appeared to the shepherds to tell them that a King was born.

e. The ____agnus____ was asleep on the hillside.

4. Start practicing "Joy to the World" in Latin (found on page 70).

Show What You Know

Connect the English words to the Latin words.

1. **stella** — star
2. **infans** — baby
3. **pastor** — lamb
4. **agnus** — shepherd
5. **angelus** — angel

Review Words

Circle the English word that best matches the Latin word.

1. **ursa**   (bear)   bird   lion
2. **leo**   bear   bird   (lion)

Circle your answer.

3. Which Latin word did "infant" come from?   **stella**   **pastor**   (**infans**)
4. Which Latin word did "constellation" come from?   (**stella**)   **mater**   **agnus**

Chapter 17   More Christmas Words

Words to Learn

1. **cano**   I sing
2. **laudo**   I praise
3. **do**   I give
4. **donum**   gift

Chapter Song

<u>Christmas Chant (Continued)</u> [Track 18(C)/48(E)]

Cano – I sing,
On Christmas day,
Do a donum – in a cheerful way.

Donum – present,
Do – I give,
Laudo – every day I live.

Chapter Lesson

We have more words this week that make us think about Christmas. Look at your new words and ask yourself if they are things you can touch. **Donum** is a noun, because you can certainly touch a present. Three of your new words, though, are not nouns, because they are things you do. They are actions. Anything that you do is named by a verb. Verbs are words that describe actions. "I sing" is doing something, so it is a verb. What are the other two verbs?

These three verbs have the special ending on them that means "I." What is the letter on the end of each one? Yes – *o* is the special ending that means "I."

<u>Famous Latin Saying</u>

Vergil is a famous Roman writer who wrote a book called the *Aeneid* (ay-NEE-id). It features the hero Aeneas (ay-NEE-as) who travels from Troy to start the city of Rome. The first line of this famous book is **arma virumque cano**—"of arms and the man I sing." The man that Vergil will be singing or writing about is Aeneas!

Grow Your English

Do and **donum** give us the English word "donation." A donation is just a gift. It usually means a gift given for a special cause. Do you see the Latin hidden in the beginning of the word or the end of the word?

Practice Your Latin

1. Practice writing your new words by tracing the dots.

Cano Laudo Do Donum

2. In the box to the right, draw a picture of a **donum** under a Christmas tree.

3. Fill in the sentences with the Latin word that fits best.

a. _____Cano_____ songs whenever I am happy.

b. _____Do_____ presents to my friends.

c. I want to give a special _____donum_____ to my mom.

d. _____Laudo_____ the beautiful present I received.

4. Make a Christmas card and use Latin words. One way you can do this is to draw a Christmas picture and label the things that you know in Latin.

Show What You Know

Match the Latin words to the English words.

1. **do** — I sing
2. **donum** — gift
3. **cano** — I praise
4. **laudo** — I give

Review Words

Circle the English word that best matches the Latin word.

1. **stella**   (star)   shepherd   gift
2. **pastor**   star   (shepherd)   gift

Chapter 18   Review

Chapter 14 Words

1. **canis**   dog
2. **feles**   cat
3. **equus**   horse
4. **piscis**   fish

Chapter 15 Words

1. **leo**   lion
2. **avis**   bird
3. **ursa**   bear
4. **elephantus**   elephant

Chapter 16 Words

1. **angelus**   angel
2. **pastor**   shepherd
3. **agnus**   lamb
4. **stella**   star
5. **infans**   baby

Chapter 17 Words

1. **do** _____I give_____
2. **donum** _____gift_____
3. **cano** _____I sing_____
4. **laudo** _____I praise_____

Master Your Songs

<u>Animal Song</u> [Tracks 15-16(C)/45-46(E)]

Listen to the **canis** early in the morning,
Barking at the **feles** and makin' her run away.
"Meow" said the **feles** and went to catch a **piscis**,
And she climbed on an **equus** munching on his hay.
Neigh, neigh! Meow, meow! Off we go!

See the little **avis** flying 'round the **leo**,
"Roar" says the **leo** and scares away the bird.
Along comes the **ursa** and eats up all the honey,
Elephantus stomps around his little elephant herd.
Tweet, tweet! Roar, roar! Off we go!

<u>Christmas Chant</u> [Tracks 17-18(C)/47-48(E)]

Angelus – angel,
Stella – star,
Both appeared in the sky afar.

Pastor – shepherd,
Agnus – lamb,
Shepherds watching the little lambs.
Infans – baby,
Born in the hay,
Jesus, born on Christmas day.
Cano – I sing,
On Christmas day,
Do a donum – in a cheerful way.
Donum – present,
Do – I give,
Laudo – every day I live.

<u>Joy to the World</u> *(Here is an additional song for you to pratice.)*
Laetissimus, Accipiat, Iam mundus Dominum.
Dum omnia in corda nos,
Accipimus illum,
Accipimus illum,
Accip-, accipimus, illum.

Activities

1. Circle your answers.

   a. Which animal can fly?   elephantus   (avis)   leo

   b. Which of these animals is the heaviest?   canis   feles   (elephantus)

   c. Which one of these animals lives in the water? (piscis)   ursa   equus

   d. Which one of these animals does a cowboy ride? feles   (equus)   leo

   e. What do you get on your birthday?   elephantus   (donum)   ursa

f. If you are in a choir, what do you do? (cano) canis do

g. Who watches the sheep in the field? do (pastor) infans

h. Who came to tell the shepherds about the birth of Jesus? ursa equus (angelus)

i. Jesus came to earth as a tiny _____. (infans) cano angelus

2. Put all of the animals back in their proper places! Color each animal and draw a line to their proper cage.

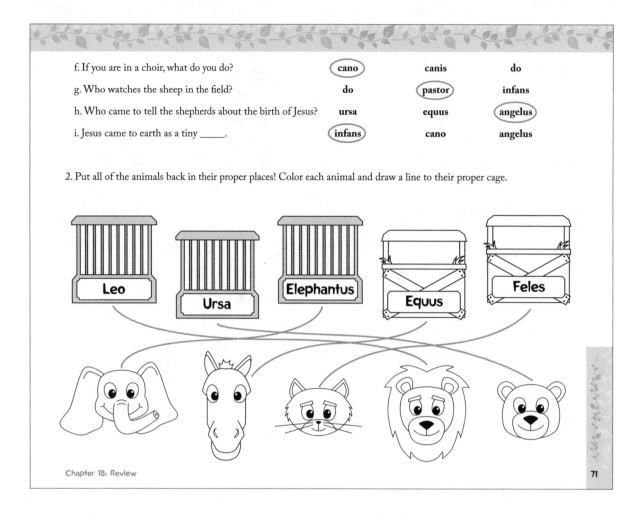

Chapter Story

Christmas Announcement

On a cold night, long ago, there were **pastores** out on a hillside watching their **agnos**. It was quiet and dark, and the **agni** were asleep. All of a sudden, an **angelus** appeared in the sky with a host of other **angeli**. The **pastores** were very afraid! But the **angelus** said, "Don't be afraid! I have wonderful news!" And the **angelus** told them that Jesus the Savior was born that night and told them that they would find the **infans** Jesus in a barn, sleeping in a manger. Then many **angeli** appeared

with him and sang "Glory to God!" The **pastores** were so excited that they left the **agnos** and went to find the **infans** Jesus. They found him in a barn, with Mary and Joseph, as the **angelus** said. Each shepherd bowed down in worship and praise.

Later, the Wise Men came to see the **infans** Jesus, too. They saw a bright **stella** in the sky. They followed the **stella** to Jesus, and they each brought a precious **donum** to him. "**Donum Iesu do**," said the first wise man as he gave gold to Jesus. The second wise man gave Jesus frankincense and the third gave him myrrh.

Words to Learn

1. **manus**   hand
2. **pes**   foot
3. **caput**   head
4. **corpus**   body

Chapter Song

<u>Action Song</u> [Track 19(C)/49(E)]

If you're happy and you know it, wave your hand – **man-us**!
If you're happy and you know it, wave your hand – **man-us**!
If you're happy and you know it, then your face will surely show it,
If you're happy and you know it, wave your hand – **man-us**!

If you're happy and you know it, stomp your foot – **pes, pes**!
If you're happy and you know it, stomp your foot – **pes, pes**!
If you're happy and you know it, then your face will surely show it,
If you're happy and you know it, stomp your foot – **pes, pes**!

If you're happy and you know it, nod your head – **ca-put**!
If you're happy and you know it, nod your head – **ca-put**!
If you're happy and you know it, then your face will surely show it,
If you're happy and you know it, nod your head – **ca-put**!

If you're happy and you know it, spin around – **cor-pus**!
If you're happy and you know it, spin around – **cor-pus**!
If you're happy and you know it, then your face will surely show it,
If you're happy and you know it, spin around – **cor-pus**!

73

Chapter Lesson

Isn't your body (**corpus**) wonderfully put together? Think of all the things that you can do with the parts of your **corpus** that you are learning in Latin this week. You can draw with your **manus**, or hop on your **pes**. Try to use your new words often. It's really fun to walk up to your friend and say, "There's an **avis** on your **caput**!" or, "Let me shake your **manus**!" See how many times you can use your new words in conversation this week.

<u>Famous Latin Saying</u>

In a country where the people can vote, they can have a "voice" in deciding who will be the leader or president. Once a president has been elected, we can say that the **vox populi**, "the voice of the people," has been heard.

Grow Your English

There are many English words that come from the Latin words for hand and foot. "Manuscript" means "written by hand." "Manual" means that you have to do it "by hand." You can guess which Latin word they came from! A "pedestrian" is someone who is "on foot." If you are riding on a bike or in a car, you are not a pedestrian. Whenever you are walking on your feet, though, you are. You can see the Latin word for foot right in the beginning of the word.

> **Teacher's Notes**
>
> Additional Activity: Each student colors, cuts out and labels a picture of a hand, foot, body, and head to hold up when the teacher says the Latin words. There are lots of game possibilities with this!

Practice Your Latin

1. Practice writing your new words by tracing the dots.

Manus Pes Caput Corpus

Chapter 19: The Body

Song School Latin Teacher's Edition

2. Using the picture to the right, follow the instrustions below.

   a. Draw a hat on the boy's **caput**. (head)

   b. Draw boots on the boy's **pes**. (feet)

   c. Draw a coat on the boy's **corpus**. (body)

   d. Draw gloves on the boy's **manus**. (hands)

3. Circle your answer to complete each sentence.

a. Kick the ball with your:	manus	corpus	leo	**(pes)**
b. Put your hat on your:	pes	corpus	agnus	**(caput)**
c. Please raise your _____ before you speak!	caput	stella	**(manus)**	pes
d. My whole _____ has many parts!	manus	pes	**(corpus)**	caput

Show What You Know

Match the Latin words to their English meanings.

1. **manus**   foot
2. **corpus**   hand
3. **pes**   head
4. **caput**   body

Review

Match the Latin words to their English meanings.

1. **liber**   pencil
2. **agnus**   baby
3. **stylus**   book
4. **infans**   lamb

The Face Chapter 20

Words to Learn

1. **auris** ear
2. **nares** nose
3. **oculus** eye
4. **os** mouth

Chapter Song

<u>Action Song (Continued)</u> [Track 20(C)/50(E)]

If you're happy and you know it, touch your nose – **na-res**!
If you're happy and you know it, touch your nose – **na-res**!
If you're happy and you know it, then your face will surely show it,
If you're happy and you know it, touch your nose – **na-res**!

If you're happy and you know it, tug your ear – **au-ris**!
If you're happy and you know it, tug your ear – **au-ris**!
If you're happy and you know it, then your face will surely show it,
If you're happy and you know it, tug your ear – **au-ris**!

If you're happy and you know it, wink your eye – **oculus**!
If you're happy and you know it, wink your eye – **oculus**!
If you're happy and you know it, then your face will surely show it,
If you're happy and you know it, wink your eye – **oculus**!

If you're happy and you know it, close your mouth – **os, os**! (finger to lips)
If you're happy and you know it, close your mouth – **os, os**!
If you're happy and you know it, then your face will surely show it,
If you're happy and you know it, close your mouth – **os, os**!

77

Chapter Lesson

The new words in this chapter are naming the parts of you that help you discover and explore things around you. Your **oculus** allows you to see things. Your **nares** allows you to smell things. Your **auris** allows you to hear things, and your **os** allows you to taste things, as well as speak. These are called your "senses." These parts of you also allow you to make all kinds of interesting expressions! Wrinkle your **nares** and open your **os** wide.

<u>Famous Latin Saying</u>

Look at the words **vox populi**. Can you see how easily our English word "voice" comes from **vox**? We also get our word "vocal" from **vox**. Do you know what your vocal cords are? Can you see that our word "people" comes from **populi**? We also get our word "population" from **populi**.

Grow Your English

Binoculars. There really is a Latin word in there that you know! Binoculars are like extra power for your eyes so that you can see things far away. You look through binoculars with your eyes. Look at the part of the word after "bin" and you can see part of the Latin word for "eye."

> **Teacher's Notes**
> Additional Activity: Each student colors, cuts out and labels a picture of a mouth, head, ear, and nose to hold up when the teacher says the Latin words.

Practice Your Latin

1. Practice writing your new words by tracing the dots.

Auris Nares Oculus Os

2. Make lunch bag puppets and glue on the facial features labeled in Latin.

3. Play "Simon Says!" using vocabulary from Chapters 19 to 20.

Song School Latin Teacher's Edition

43

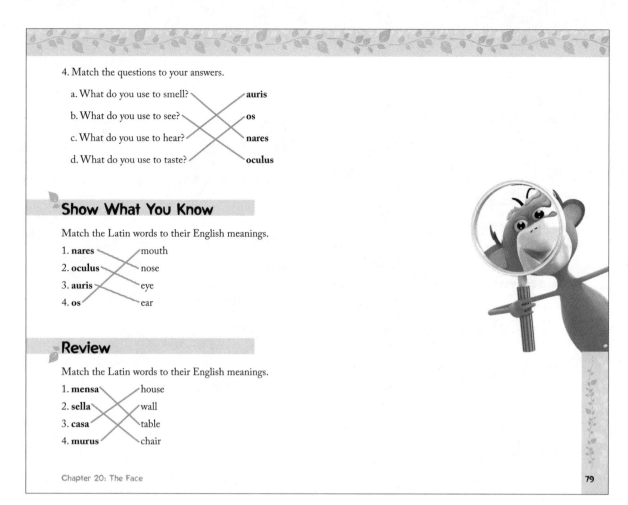

4. Match the questions to your answers.

a. What do you use to smell?   **auris**

b. What do you use to see?   **os**

c. What do you use to hear?   **nares**

d. What do you use to taste?   **oculus**

Show What You Know

Match the Latin words to their English meanings.

1. **nares**   mouth
2. **oculus**   nose
3. **auris**   eye
4. **os**   ear

Review

Match the Latin words to their English meanings.

1. **mensa**   house
2. **sella**   wall
3. **casa**   table
4. **murus**   chair

Chapter 20: The Face

79

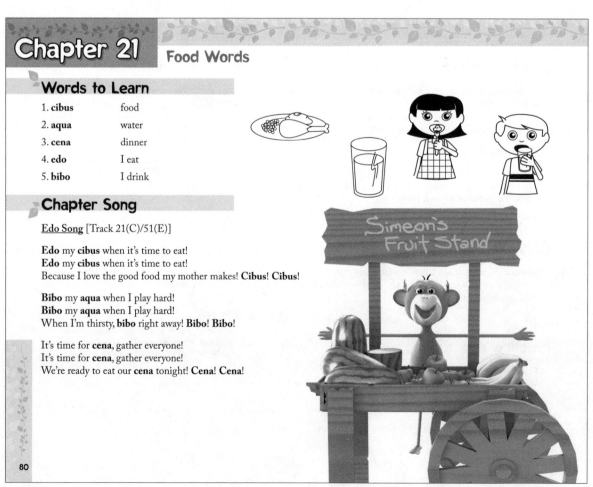

Chapter 21   Food Words

Words to Learn

1. **cibus**	food
2. **aqua**	water
3. **cena**	dinner
4. **edo**	I eat
5. **bibo**	I drink

Chapter Song

<u>Edo Song</u> [Track 21(C)/51(E)]

Edo my **cibus** when it's time to eat!
Edo my **cibus** when it's time to eat!
Because I love the good food my mother makes! **Cibus! Cibus!**

Bibo my **aqua** when I play hard!
Bibo my **aqua** when I play hard!
When I'm thirsty, **bibo** right away! **Bibo! Bibo!**

It's time for **cena**, gather everyone!
It's time for **cena**, gather everyone!
We're ready to eat our **cena** tonight! **Cena! Cena!**

Chapter Lesson

This week, you get to learn words about food and eating! There are a lot of ways you can use these words every day. Be careful not to confuse **cibus** and **cena**. They look and sound similar. There are nouns and verbs in your new word list. Can you tell which ones are verbs? Remember that verbs are action words, things that you do. How many nouns are there?

<u>Famous Latin Saying</u>

You will hear people say "**et cetera**" (meaning "and others") a lot. It is one of those Latin phrases that is used a lot in English. In writing, it abbreviated as "etc." You can use this phrase whenever you want to say "and others" or "and other things." For example, you could say, "At the picnic, we served hot dogs, hamburgers, watermelon, pies, cakes, et cetera."

Grow Your English

Have you ever visited a big aquarium? Do you have a little aquarium in your home? An aquarium is a place where people keep fish and other sea creatures. They hold water, because fish need water to live. Look at the first half of the word "aquarium" and find the Latin word in it!

Practice Your Latin

1. Practice writing your new words by tracing the dots.

Cibus Aqua Cena Edo Bibo

2. Draw a line from these Latin words to the matching picture.

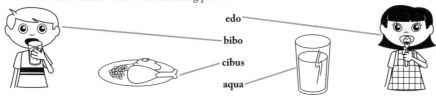

edo
bibo
cibus
aqua

3. Read or listen to the sentence and circle your answer.

a. _____ french fries when we go out to eat. (edo) bibo cena

b. We eat _____ at six o'clock. aqua cibus (cena)

c. My favorite _____ is cookies. bibo (cibus) aqua

d. Drink a lot of _____ every day! cena edo (aqua)

e. _____ orange juice in the morning. (bibo) cena cibus

Show What You Know

Match the Latin words to the English meaning.

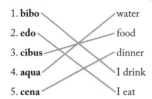

1. **bibo** water
2. **edo** food
3. **cibus** dinner
4. **aqua** I drink
5. **cena** I eat

Review

Match the Latin words to the English meaning.

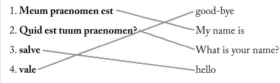

1. **Meum praenomen est** good-bye
2. **Quid est tuum praenomen?** My name is
3. **salve** What is your name?
4. **vale** hello

Words to Learn

1. **panis**   bread
2. **fructus**   fruit
3. **lac**   milk
4. **crustulum** cookie
5. **pullus**   chicken

Chapter Song

<u>Cibus Chant</u> [Track 22(C)/52(E)]

Panis—bread. (clap-clap-clap)
Panis—bread. (clap-clap-clap)

Fructus—fruit. (stomp-stomp-stomp)
Fructus—fruit. (stomp-stomp-stomp)

Lac—milk. (clap-clap-clap)
Lac—milk. (clap-clap-clap)

Crustulum—cookie. (stomp-stomp-stomp)
Crustulum—cookie. (stomp-stomp-stomp)

Pullus—chicken. (clap-clap)
Pullus—chicken. (clap-clap)

83

Chapter Lesson

Last week you learned words about eating; this week you are learning the words for five things that you eat. You drink **lac**, though, of course! Which one in the list is your favorite? You might eat your **pullus** in little nuggets, but **pullus** is also what you call a chicken that is alive. So, you can add one more animal word to your list! What is your favorite kind of **crustulum**? Do you have any **panis** in your lunchbox or pantry? Is a banana a **fructus** or a **crustulum**?

<u>Famous Latin Saying</u>

Can you create a sentence in which you use the phrase **et cetera**? Remember, you can abbreviate **et cetera** by simply writing "etc." Here is an example: "For dinner we will have **pullus, panis, fructus, crustulum,** etc." This sentence would mean: "For dinner we will have chicken, bread, fruit, a cookie, and other things."

Grow Your English

The pantry is where you keep food, or "your daily bread." Look at the beginning of the word; can you guess which Latin word it came from?

Practice Your Latin

1. Practice writing your new words by tracing the dots.

Panis   Fructus   Lac
Crustulum   Pullus

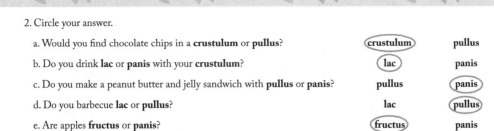

2. Circle your answer.

    a. Would you find chocolate chips in a **crustulum** or **pullus**?   (crustulum)   pullus

    b. Do you drink **lac** or **panis** with your **crustulum**?   (lac)   panis

    c. Do you make a peanut butter and jelly sandwich with **pullus** or **panis**?   pullus   (panis)

    d. Do you barbecue **lac** or **pullus**?   lac   (pullus)

    e. Are apples **fructus** or **panis**?   (fructus)   panis

3. Cut out and color the food shapes. Label them with the right Latin words! When your teacher calls out the Latin words, hold up the right picture! Save your cutouts for other games. (See page 131 for larger cutouts.)

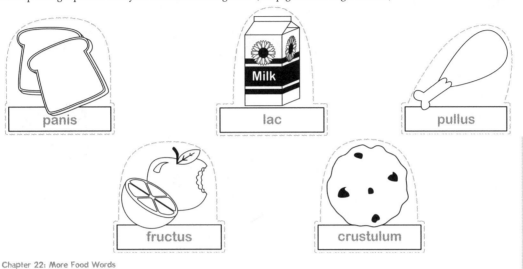

panis   lac   pullus

fructus   crustulum

Chapter 22: More Food Words   85

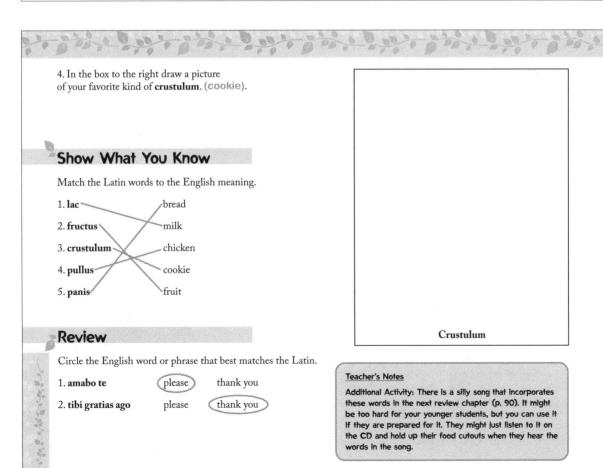

4. In the box to the right draw a picture of your favorite kind of **crustulum**. (cookie).

Show What You Know

Match the Latin words to the English meaning.

1. **lac**   bread

2. **fructus**   milk

3. **crustulum**   chicken

4. **pullus**   cookie

5. **panis**   fruit

Crustulum

Review

Circle the English word or phrase that best matches the Latin.

1. **amabo te**   (please)   thank you

2. **tibi gratias ago**   please   (thank you)

Teacher's Notes

Additional Activity: There is a silly song that incorporates these words in the next review chapter (p. 90). It might be too hard for your younger students, but you can use it if they are prepared for it. They might just listen to it on the CD and hold up their food cutouts when they hear the words in the song.

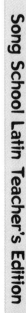

Song School Latin Teacher's Edition   47

Chapter 19 Words

1. **manus**   hand
2. **pes**   foot
3. **caput**   head
4. **corpus**   body

Chapter 20 Words

1. **auris**   ear
2. **nares**   nose
3. **oculus**   eye
4. **os**   mouth

Chapter 21 Words

1. **cibus**   food
2. **aqua**   water
3. **cena**   dinner
4. **edo**   I eat
5. **bibo**   I drink

87

Chapter 22 Words

1. **panis**   bread
2. **fructus**   fruit
3. **lac**   milk
4. **crustulum**   cookie
5. **pullus**   chicken

Master Your Songs

<u>Action Song</u> [Tracks 19-20(C)/49-50(E)]
Here is a condensed version. Watch your teacher's motions carefully so you will know what the next line is.

If you're happy and you know it, wave your hand – **man-us**!
If you're happy and you know it, stomp your foot – **pes, pes**!
If you're happy and you know it, then your face will surely show it,
If you're happy and you know it, nod your head – **ca-put**!

If you're happy and you know it, spin around – **cor-pus**!
If you're happy and you know it, touch your nose – **na-res**!
If you're happy and you know it, then your face will surely show it,
If you're happy and you know it, tug your ear – **au-ris**!

If you're happy and you know it, wink your eye – **oculus**!
If you're happy and you know it, close your mouth – **os, os**!
If you're happy and you know it, then your face will surely show it,
If you're happy and you know it, wave your hand – **man-us**!

Edo Song [Track 21(C)/51(E)]

Edo my **cibus** when it's time to eat!
Edo my **cibus** when it's time to eat!
Because I love the good food that my mother makes! **Cibus! Cibus!**

Bibo my **aqua** when I play hard!
Bibo my **aqua** when I play hard!
When I'm thirsty, **bibo** right away! **Bibo! Bibo!**

It's time for **cena**, gather everyone!
It's time for **cena**, gather everyone!
We're ready to eat our **cena** tonight! **Cena! Cena!**

Cibus Chant [Track 22(C)/52(E)]

Here is a silly chant about food that you can sing or just listen to. Listen for the Latin words!

Panis—bread. (clap-clap-clap)
Panis—bread. (clap-clap-clap)

Fructus—fruit. (stomp-stomp-stomp)
Fructus—fruit. (stomp-stomp-stomp)

Lac—milk. (clap-clap-clap)
Lac—milk. (clap-clap-clap)

Crustulum—cookie. (stomp-stomp-stomp)
Crustulum—cookie. (stomp-stomp-stomp)

Pullus—chicken. (clap-clap)
Pullus—chicken. (clap-clap)

Milk

Canis Song [Track 23(C)/53(E)]

There once was a **canis** who loved to eat bread.
He liked to speak Latin and stand on his head.
He learned to say "**panis**" and "**amabo te**."
If you say the same you can eat bread today.
Say, **panis, amabo te**, please pass the bread.

This **canis**, he also loved cookies with milk;
The other dogs didn't like dogs of his ilk.
But if he had **lac** and a big **crustulum**,
He didn't much care who hung out in his room.
Say, **lac** and a **crustulum**, cookies and milk.

They served him his dinner of chicken and fruit,
He picked up his trumpet and started to toot.
It turns out he doesn't like **pullus** at all,
And he thought that the **fructus** was his rubber ball.
Say, **pullus** is chicken and **fructus** is fruit.

Activities

* 1. Play "Simon Says" using words from this review chapter.

2. In the box to the right, draw a picture of yourself and draw a line from each Latin word to that part of you.

manus

pes

caput

nares

os

oculus

auris

Teacher's Notes

*You may use all classroom commands that students have learned in Latin, as well as parts of the body (e.g., touch your caput, etc.).

3. Fill in the matching Latin words for the sentences below, choosing from this list: **oculus**, **auris**, **os**, **nares**.

This horse has a big ___nares___ ! This cat is twitching her ___auris___ ! This bear is winking his ___oculus___ !

4. What is your favorite kind of **fructus**?
Draw a picture of it on the plate.

Teacher's Notes

*Use all the foods and fruits students have learned so far. If you want to really mix things up, you may even include cutouts that are not foods. For an extra challenge, make your own cutouts without Latin labels.

* 5. It's time to make Silly Sandwiches! Take out your food cutouts from Chapter 22 and put them on the table in front of you. Listen carefully to your teacher's instructions. When she asks you to find a specific food, take it and put it on your "sandwich". When she says: **"surgite,"** stand up and wait for your teacher to check to make sure that you have all the parts of your "sandwich" in the correct order. If you do, you may "eat" your sandwich. If they are not in the correct order, you must put them back in the pile and start over. Whoever has "eaten" all of their food pieces first wins.

6. Your mother wrote her shopping list in Latin! Draw a line from the pictures to each item on the list.

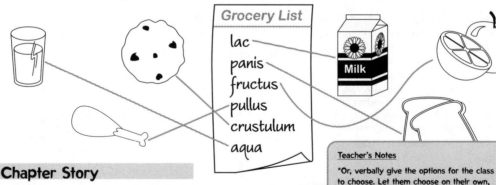

Grocery List
lac
panis
fructus
pullus
crustulum
aqua

Teacher's Notes

*Or, verbally give the options for the class to choose. Let them choose on their own, call on individual students to answer, or let them figure it out as a class.

Chapter Story

* *Follow along as your teacher reads, and circle the best answer for each blank.*

<u>Cena Time!</u>

"It's almost time for **canis / cena!**" said **Mater**. "Help me set the **mensa / nares, amabo te**. Wash up first." The **equus / puella** quickly washed up and helped her **mater**. **Mater** put the **cibus / feles** on the **mensa / murus** and said, "Call your **pater** and **frater** for **cena!**" **Pater** and **frater** washed up and then sat down in their **sella / fenestra**. "Pass the **pullus / puer, amabo te**," he said. **Frater** said, "**Edo** my **panis / auris** first!" The **puella** said "**Bibo** my **lac / fructus** first, but I will save some for my **feles / stylus** to drink." **Frater** took another piece of **edo / panis** "Close your **os / caput** when you eat, **amabo te!**" said **Mater**. "When you clean up your plates, we will have a **aqua / crustulum** for dessert." "Yum!" said the **puella**, "**Edo** my **pullus / pes** quickly!" When they finished eating, everyone helped to clear the dishes and the **fenestra / cibus** off of the table. "**Tibi gratias ago** for making a good **cena / nares!**" said **Pater**.

Weather — Chapter 24

Words to Learn

1. **nix** — snow
2. **imber** — rain
3. **ventus** — wind
4. **nimbus** — cloud
5. **arcus** — rainbow

Chapter Song

<u>Weather Song</u> [Track 24(C)/54(E)]

In the springtime,
When the rain comes,
Use your umbrella in the **imber**.
When the **ventus** blows,
And it's nipping at your nose,
Come inside out of the weather.

After rainstorms,
After **imber**,
Sometimes you see a pretty rainbow.
If you look up high,
There's an **arcus** in the sky,
The whole earth is glowing with a rainbow.

In the winter,
When the snow comes,
Nix covers everything in sight.
And the clouds are gray,
Every **nimbus** comes to play,
A **nix-nimbus** makes the world white.

93

Chapter Lesson

This week you will learn words about the weather. They are all nouns. Do you get much **nix** where you live? Name some of the fun things you can do in the **nix**. Have you ever seen a double **arcus**? Do you ever see shapes in a **nimbus**? Which one of your new Latin words best describes the weather today?

<u>Famous Latin Saying</u>

Festina lente, "make haste slowly," is a good phrase for students to learn well. It means that the best way to speed ahead is often to go slowly. In other words you will get work done fastest if you take your time and do it correctly so you don't have to do it again! Have you ever tried to do something too fast and then made a mistake so that you had to start all over again?

Practice Your Latin

1. Practice writing your new words by tracing the dots.

Nix Imber Ventus Nimbus Arcus

2. Using the pictures below, follow these instructions: a) Draw the things on the **puer** that he might need to go out in the **imber**; b) Draw the things on the **puella** that she might need to go out in the **nix**.

(Answers will vary.)
<u>Suggestions:</u>
coat
hat
gloves
snow boots
scarf

(Answers will vary.)
<u>Suggestions:</u>
umbrella
raincoat
rain hat
rubber boots

94

Chapter 24: Weather

* 4. Color and cut out the rain, snowflake, rainbow, cloud, and wind and label them with the Latin names. Hold up the right shape when your teacher calls out the Latin words!

> **Teacher's Notes**
> *Put larger versions of these on classroom walls.
> Additional Activity: Have your students give "weather reports" using their new Latin words.

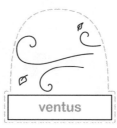

ventus

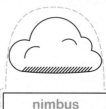

nimbus

Show What You Know

Match the Latin words to English words.

1. **nix** — cloud
2. **imber** — snow
3. **arcus** — wind
4. **nimbus** — rainbow
5. **ventus** — rain

nix

Review

Match the Latin words to English words.

1. **mensa** — book
2. **liber** — write
3. **sede** — rise/stand up
4. **surge** — table
5. **scribe** — sit down

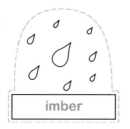

imber

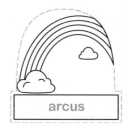

arcus

Chapter 24: Weather

95

Chapter 25   The Seasons

Words to Learn

1. **hiems**   winter
2. **ver**   spring
3. **autumnus**   fall
4. **aestas**   summer

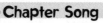

Chapter Song

<u>Seasons Song</u> [Track 25(C)/55(E)]

A gust of fall wind, blowing leaves,
Tells me that **autumnus** is here.
The white **nix** covers each blade of grass,
And I know that the **hiems** is drawing near.

The spring flowers bloom and grass turns green,
I see that the **ver** is on its way.
The sun beats down on the summer fields,
For the **aestas** has come with a sunny day.

Chapter Lesson

Last week you learned words about the weather. Weather changes with the seasons in most places. This week you will learn the Latin words for the four seasons. Do you have a favorite season? There is something special and beautiful about each one.

<u>Famous Latin Saying</u>

Festina Lente ("make haste slowly." **Festina** means "make haste" and **lente** means "slowly.") You will "make haste" or go quickly when you slow down enough to do something correctly. The famous American named Benjamin Franklin once said that "Haste makes waste." This week try not to go so fast that you make needless mistakes that end up taking up even more of your time!

Song School Latin Teacher's Edition

Grow Your English

Autumnus looks very much like autumn, doesn't it? You have probably heard that word; "autumn" is another English word for "fall." Can you guess where we got it from?

Practice Your Latin

1. Practice writing your new words by tracing the dots.

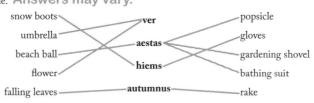

2. In which season do you usually use or see these items? Connect each of these items listed on the left and right to the seasons listed in the middle. Answers may vary.

snow boots — **ver** — popsicle
umbrella — gloves
beach ball — **aestas** — gardening shovel
flower — **hiems** — bathing suit
falling leaves — **autumnus** — rake

3. Circle a Latin word to complete each sentence.

a. I like to go sledding in the _____.	(hiems)	ver	autumnus	aestas
b. I rake leaves in the _____.	hiems	ver	(autumnus)	aestas
c. _____ is the best time for swimming.	hiems	ver	autumnus	(aestas)
d. Flowers start blooming in the _____.	hiems	(ver)	autumnus	aestas
e. Leaves turn pretty colors in the _____.	hiems	ver	(autumnus)	aestas
f. Christmas comes in the _____.	(hiems)	ver	autumnus	aestas

Chapter 25: The Seasons

97

4. Draw a picture of your favorite thing to do in each season. If you like to swim in the summer, you could draw a pool; if you like to sled in the winter, you could draw a sled. Use your imagination!

(spring)	(summer)	(fall)	(winter)
Ver	Aestas	Autumnus	Hiems

Show What You Know

Circle the Latin word that best matches the English word.

1. winter	(hiems)	ver	autumnus	aestas
2. spring	hiems	(ver)	autumnus	aestas
3. fall	hiems	ver	(autumnus)	aestas
4. summer	hiems	ver	autumnus	(aestas)

Review

Circle the English word or phrase that best matches the Latin.

1. **Quid agis?**	hello	well/fine	(How are you?)
2. **bene**	great	(well/fine)	terrible
3. **optime**	terrible	good-bye	(great)

98

Chapter 25: The Seasons

Song School Latin Teacher's Edition 53

The Sky Chapter 26

Words to Learn

1. **caelum**   sky
2. **luna**   moon
3. **stella**   star
4. **sol**   sun

Chapter Song

<u>Caelum Song</u> [Track 26(C)/56(E)]

Luna moon and **stella** star,
How I wonder what you are.
Up above in the **caelum** high,
Like a diamond in the sky.
When the nighttime turns to day,
Then the **sol** comes out to stay.

Chapter Lesson

This week you will learn four words about the sky. One of them you already know – **stella**! This should be an easy chapter to master. Try to go out and look at the **luna** and **stellas** up in the **caelum** this week!

99

<u>Famous Latin Saying</u>

E pluribus unum—"out of many, one." This is the motto on the Great Seal of the United States. People came out of many different nations to form one new nation—The United States. The words **e pluribus** mean "out of many" (many nations or peoples). The word **unum** means "one." Though there are many stars, there is only one…**caelum**.

Grow Your English

A lunar shuttle goes to the moon on a lunar mission. "Lunar" comes from one of your new Latin words. Which one does it sound like? luna

Practice Your Latin

> **Teacher's Notes**
> Additional Activity: post large night sky and day sky pictures on the wall and let each student put up their own stella, luna, sol.

1. Practice writing your new words by tracing the dots.

Caelum Luna Stella Sol

2. Cut out and color the **luna**, **sol**, **nimbus**, and **stellas**. Label them each with the right Latin words. Turn to page 137 and paste them to the matching **caelum**. (See page 135 for larger cutouts.)

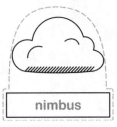

nimbus

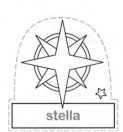

stella

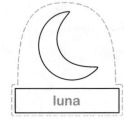

luna

sol

Chapter 26: The Sky

100

Song School Latin Teacher's Edition

54

3. Circle your answer to complete the sentence.

a. The _____ shines when it is day.   luna   (sol)   caelum

b. The cow jumped over the _____!   (luna)   stella   sol

c. I saw a falling _____ in the sky.   caelum   (stella)   sol

d. The airplane took off into the _____.   luna   stella   (caelum)

Show What You Know

Match the Latin word to the English word.

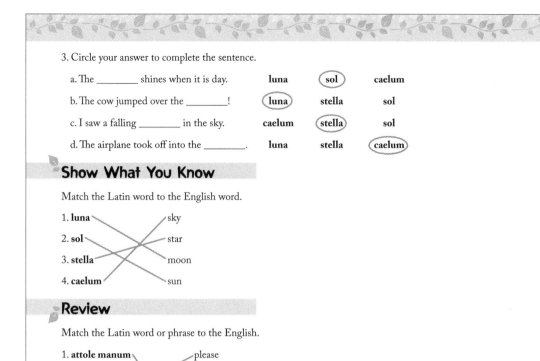

1. **luna** — moon

2. **sol** — sun

3. **stella** — star

4. **caelum** — sky

Review

Match the Latin word or phrase to the English.

1. **attole manum** — raise your hand

2. **audi** — listen

3. **amabo te** — please

4. **tace** — be quiet

5. **ignosce mihi** — excuse me

Chapter 26: The Sky

101

Chapter 27   Review

Chapter 24 Words

1. nix — snow

2. imber — rain

3. ventus — wind

4. nimbus — cloud

5. arcus — rainbow

Chapter 25 Words

1. hiems — winter

2. ver — spring

3. autumnus — fall

4. aestas — summer

Chapter 26 Words

1. caelum — sky

2. luna — moon

3. stella — star

4. sol — sun

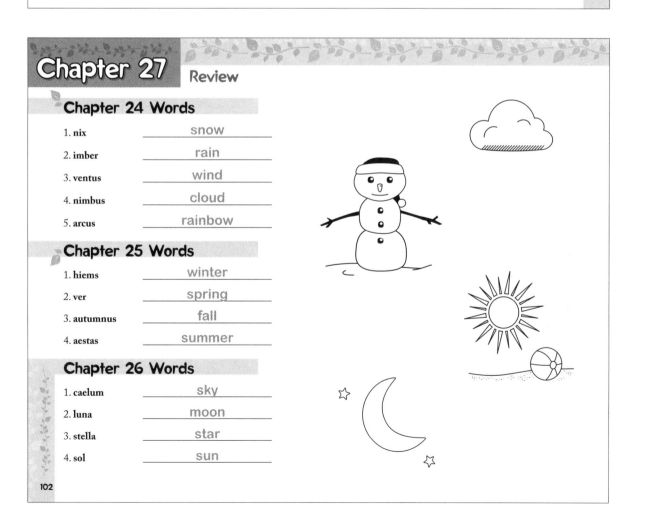

Master Your Songs

<u>Weather Song</u> [Track 24(C)/54(E)]

In the springtime,
When the rain comes,
Use your umbrella in the **imber**.
When the **ventus** blows,
And it's nipping at your nose,
Come inside out of the weather.

After rainstorms,
After **imber**,
Sometimes you see a pretty rainbow.
If you look up high,
There's an **arcus** in the sky,
The whole earth is glowing with a rainbow.

In the winter,
When the snow comes,
Nix covers everything in sight.
And the clouds are gray,
Every **nimbus** comes to play,
A **nix-nimbus** makes the world white.

<u>Seasons Song</u> [Track 25(C)/55(E)]

A gust of fall wind, blowing leaves,
Tells me that **autumnus** is here.
The white **nix** covers each blade of grass,
And I know that the **hiems** is drawing near.

The spring flowers bloom and grass turns green,
I see that the **ver** is on its way.
The sun beats down on the summer fields,
For the **aestas** has come with a sunny day.

<u>Caelum Song</u> [Track 26(C)/56(E)]

Luna moon and **stella** star,
How I wonder what you are.
Up above in the **caelum** high,
Like a diamond in the sky.
When the nighttime turns to day,
Then the **sol** comes out to stay.

Activities

1. Color each picture and add things to make it look like the right season. Think about the sky and the weather as you draw. Be ready to tell the Latin names for the things in your pictures!

Aestas   **Ver**   **Hiems**   **Autumnus**

2. Draw a line from the pictures to the Latin words.

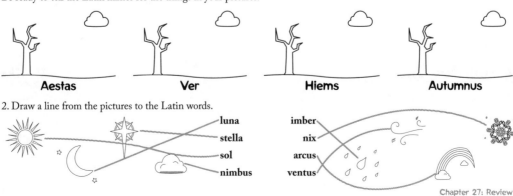

luna
stella
sol
nimbus

imber
nix
arcus
ventus

Chapter Story

<u>Joseph's Dream</u>

Once there was a **puer** named Joseph, and he lived with his eleven **fraters**. They were jealous of Joseph because he had a coat with all the colors of the **arcus**. They were mean to Joseph. One night, when everyone was in bed sleeping, Joseph had a strange dream. He dreamed that he was out in a field. It was **autumnus**, so he was harvesting wheat with his **fraters**. All of a sudden his bundle of wheat stood straight up, and his **fraters'** bundles of wheat all bowed down to his wheat! Then he had another dream. He dreamed that the **sol**, the **luna**, and eleven **stellas** all bowed down to him. When he told his dreams to his **fraters**, they were angry! "We will never bow to you like that!" they said. Even his **pater** agreed. But they were wrong.

One day, Joseph's **fraters** were so angry with him that they sold him as a slave. The slave traders took him very far away, to Egypt. Joseph was very sad and his life was very hard for a long time. Whenever he looked up in the night **caelum** and saw the **stellas** and **luna**, he remembered his dream. But he worked faithfully in the hot **sol** and **ventus**, or in the **imber**, and a few years later, Pharaoh made Joseph a very important ruler in Egypt. He was in charge of almost everything and he lived in the palace. He helped the people store up **cibus** before a famine.

One **ver** day, he saw his **fraters** coming to get **cibus**! They bowed down to him, just like the **sol**, **luna**, and **stellas** had done in Joseph's dream. Joseph forgave them for being so unkind to him. He gave them the **cibus** they needed. Soon after that, his whole family came to live with him in Egypt. They were very happy to be together again!

– Adapted from Genesis 37 & 42

> **Teacher's Notes**
> **Additional Activities:**
> 1. As a class, create wall murals/posters for each of the four seasons.
> 2. Make constellations on black or dark blue poster/construction paper.
> 3. Make mobiles for the different weather conditions; label with Latin words.

Chapter 28   Water Words

Words to Learn

1. **mare**   sea
2. **unda**   wave
3. **lacus**   lake
4. **flumen**   river
5. **navis**   ship/boat

Chapter Song

<u>Row Your Navis</u> [Track 27(C)/57(E)]

Navis, navis – boat,
Mare, mare – sea.
Ride the **unda**, ride the wave,
Happy as can be.

Lacus, lacus – lake,
Flumen – river, stream.
Row your **navis**, row your boat,
Life is but a dream.

Chapter Lesson

Did you notice that all of your new words this week are related to water? If you like boats and playing in water, you will have a lot of fun with these words! Have you ever been in a **navis**? Have you ever gone tubing on a **flumen** or fishing on a **lacus**?

Famous Latin Saying

If you live in America, do you know what country your ancestors lived in before they came to the United States? Can you tell what English word comes from **pluribus** (from Chapter 26's phrase)? The word "plural," which means many or more than one. If you add an "s" to most nouns you make it plural (like "state" and "states"). Though there are many waves, there is just one…**mare**.

Grow Your English

A navy is a part of the military that mainly operates on the water. The United States Navy has many, many ships! What Latin word do you think navy came from?

Practice Your Latin

> **Teacher's Notes**
> *This activity is a little tricky, so be ready to give students assistance.

1. Practice writing your new words by tracing the dots.

Mare Unda Lacus Flumen Navis

* 2. Turn to page 139 and follow the directions to make a **navis**. Be sure to sail it when you sing the song!

3. Using the pictures below, follow the instructions to draw the correct Latin words.

a. Draw a **piscis** in the **unda**.
(fish)   (wave)

b. Draw a bridge over the **flumen**.
(river)

c. Draw a **navis** on the **lacus**.
(ship/boat) (lake)

Chapter 28: Water Words

107

---

4. Circle the word that fits best.

a. The Nile _____ is in Egypt.   lacus   **(flumen)**   navis

b. A _____ knocked me over when I went to the ocean.   navis   **(unda)**   flumen

c. I sailed around Africa in my _____.   lacus   mare   **(navis)**

d. Seahorses live in the _____.   flumen   **(mare)**   lacus

e. The lake house is beside the _____.   **(lacus)**   unda   navis

Show What You Know

Match the Latin word to the English word.

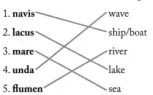

1. **navis** — ship/boat
2. **lacus** — lake
3. **mare** — sea
4. **unda** — wave
5. **flumen** — river

Review:

Match the Latin word to the English word.

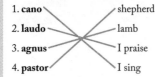

1. **cano** — I sing
2. **laudo** — I praise
3. **agnus** — lamb
4. **pastor** — shepherd

Song School Latin Teacher's Edition

58

108

Chapter 28: Water Words

Gardening

Chapter 29

Words to Learn

1. **flos**   flower
2. **herba**   plant
3. **hortus**   garden
4. **folium**   leaf
5. **humus**   ground/dirt

Chapter Song

<u>Hortus Song</u> [Track 28(C)/58(E)]

Grab your shovel,
Put your gloves on,
It's time to plant our summer **hortus**.
Here's a **herba**, plant,
With a **folium**, a leaf,
Let's plant it in our summer **hortus**.

Plant a flower,
Plant a **flos**.
Plant pretty flowers in our **hortus**,
Plant the roots deep down.
In the **humus**, in the ground,
We love to grow a summer **hortus**.

109

Chapter Lesson

Have you ever helped to plant a garden? Even if you have not, you have seen many things growing. It is amazing to see how a tiny seed can grow into a plant or a big tree, and even produce food for us to eat. Next time you go outside, notice all the things that are growing, and call as many as you can by their Latin names.

<u>Famous Latin Saying</u>

When you make a mistake, you can simply say, "Sorry, **mea culpa**!" Mea culpa means "my fault." If you accidently poured **aqua** on your **feles**, you should say "**Mea culpa!**" to your cat.

Practice Your Latin

1. Practice writing your new words by tracing the dots.

Flos Herba Hortus Folium Humus

2. Draw your garden and connect the vocabulary words to the things in your garden.

flos	herba	hortus	folium	humus
(flower)	(plant)	(garden)	(leaf)	(ground/dirt)

110   Chapter 29: Gardening

Song School Latin Teacher's Edition   59

3. Circle the word that fits best.

a. Till the _____ before you plant a garden! folium (humus) herba

b. Pick a _____ for your mother. humus herba (flos)

c. The _____ on the tree changes colors in the fall. (folium) hortus arbor

d. We grow a lot of vegetables in our _____. folium (hortus) herba

e. I pick tomatoes off of the tomato _____. humus folium (herba)

Show What You Know

Circle the correct English definition of these Latin words.

1. **hortus** (garden) plant flower

2. **herba** leaf flower (plant)

3. **humus** flower garden (ground/dirt)

4. **flos** plant (flower) leaf

5. **folium** (leaf) ground/dirt plant

Review

Circle the correct English definition of these Latin words.

1. **lacus** summer river (lake)

2. **navis** river (ship/boat) winter

3. **hiems** (winter) lake spring

4. **aestas** fall winter (summer)

Chapter 29: Gardening

Chapter 30 Playing Outdoors

Words to Learn

1. **mons** mountain
2. **arbor** tree
3. **saxum** rock
4. **collis** hill
5. **silva** forest

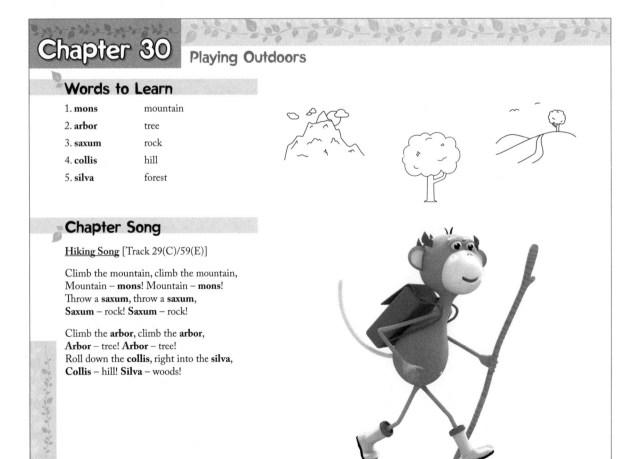

Chapter Song

<u>Hiking Song</u> [Track 29(C)/59(E)]

Climb the mountain, climb the mountain,
Mountain – **mons**! Mountain – **mons**!
Throw a **saxum**, throw a **saxum**,
Saxum – rock! **Saxum** – rock!

Climb the **arbor**, climb the **arbor**,
Arbor – tree! **Arbor** – tree!
Roll down the **collis**, right into the **silva**,
Collis – hill! **Silva** – woods!

Chapter Lesson

You have five outdoor words to learn this week. Think about and practice these words whenever you go outside! You probably at least see an **arbor** every day. You probably see a **saxum**, too. If you throw a **saxum**, make sure nothing is in the way! All of the words in this chapter are nouns. Do you remember how you find nouns that are in the first declension? (They end with an *a*.) Can you tell which of your new words is a first declension noun?

<u>Famous Latin Saying</u>

If you have ever spent a long time on a boat, it usually feels good when you finally arrive to shore and can put your feet on **terra firma**—"solid ground." People often use the phrase **terra firma** to say that something is strong and solid, even when they don't really mean the ground. For example, somone might say, "I did not understand my math homework until my sister explained it to me. Now I feel that I am on **terra firma**." From **firma** we get our word "firm."

Practice Your Latin

1. Practice writing your new words by tracing the dots.

Mons Arbor Saxum Collis Silva

2. Label your pictures with the Latin words.

a. Draw a **saxum** on a **collis**.	b. Draw an **arbor** on a **mons**.	c. Draw a **silva**.
(rock) (hill)	(tree) (mountain)	(forest)

---

* 3. Look at the pictures and fill in the correct Latin word to complete the sentences, choosing from the words in the box.

a. The  __elephantus__ is eating a **folium** from the __arbor__ .

b. The bear is hiding in the __silva__ .

> **Teacher's Notes**
> *Students who take a long time to write may just draw lines from the words to the blanks.

c. The **vir** is climbing the big __mons__ .

d. The **puer** found a new __saxum__ on the road to add to his collection.

e. The children are sledding down the __collis__ in the snow.

saxum	collis	elephantus	mons	silva	arbor

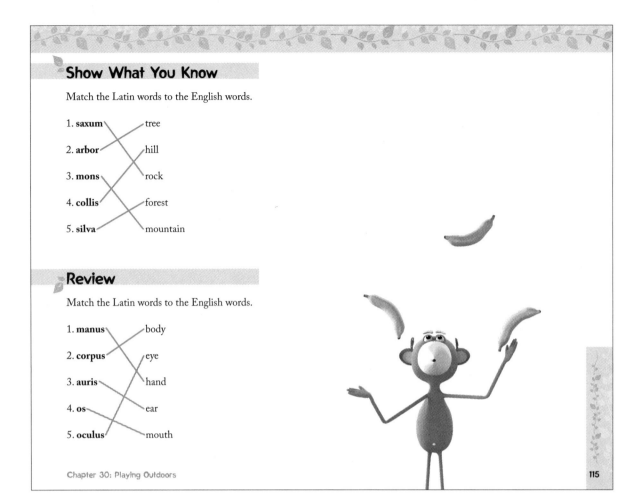

Show What You Know

Match the Latin words to the English words.

1. **saxum** — tree
2. **arbor** — hill
3. **mons** — rock
4. **collis** — forest
5. **silva** — mountain

Review

Match the Latin words to the English words.

1. **manus** — body
2. **corpus** — eye
3. **auris** — hand
4. **os** — ear
5. **oculus** — mouth

Chapter 30: Playing Outdoors

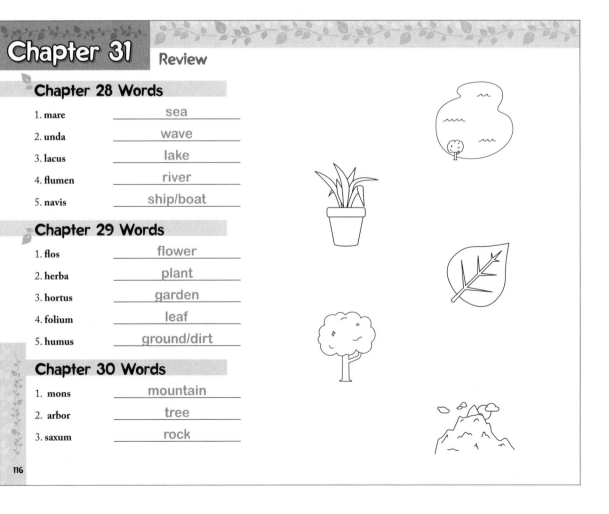

Chapter 31   Review

Chapter 28 Words

1. **mare**   sea
2. **unda**   wave
3. **lacus**   lake
4. **flumen**   river
5. **navis**   ship/boat

Chapter 29 Words

1. **flos**   flower
2. **herba**   plant
3. **hortus**   garden
4. **folium**   leaf
5. **humus**   ground/dirt

Chapter 30 Words

1. **mons**   mountain
2. **arbor**   tree
3. **saxum**   rock

4. **collis** _____hill_____

5. **silva** _____forest_____

Master Your Songs

<u>Row Your Navis</u> [Track 27(C)/57(E)]

Navis, navis – boat,
Mare, mare – sea.
Ride the **unda**, ride the wave,
Happy as can be.

Lacus, lacus – lake,
Flumen – river, stream.
Row your **navis**, row your boat,
Life is but a dream.

<u>Hortus Song</u> [Track 28(C)/58(E)]

Grab your shovel,
Put your gloves on,
It's time to plant our summer **hortus**.
Here's an **herba**, plant,
With a **folium**, a leaf,
Let's plant it in our summer **hortus**.

Plant a flower,
Plant a **flos**.
Plant pretty flowers in our **hortus**,
Plant the roots deep down.
In the **humus**, in the ground,
We love to grow a summer **hortus**.

<u>Hiking Song</u> [Track 29(C)/59(E)]

Climb the mountain, climb the mountain,
Mountain – **mons**! Mountain – **mons**!
Throw a **saxum**, throw a **saxum**,
Saxum - rock! **Saxum** – rock!

Climb the arbor, Climb the arbor,
Arbor – tree! **Arbor** – tree!
Roll down the **collis**, right into the **silva**,
Collis - hill! **Silva** – woods!

<u>Sailing Song</u> [Track 30(C)/60(E)]
Here is another song you can listen to to help you remember the water words.

As I sailed out on the wide open **mare**,
I sailed on the **mare** as free as could be.
I spied a huge **unda** about to wash o'er me,
An **unda** of **aqua** out on the wide sea.

I cast off my **navis** to fish in the **flumen**,
Fish in the **flumen** one warm summer night.
The river, it took me right out to the **lacus**,
And there on the **lacus** I got my first bite.

Activities

1. Label all the key items in this scene.

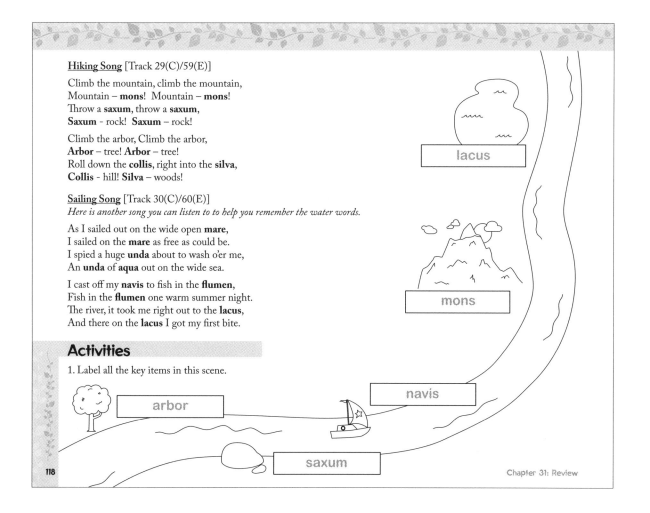

lacus

mons

navis

arbor

saxum

2. Look at the pictures and fill in the correct Latin word to complete the sentences, choosing from the words in the box.

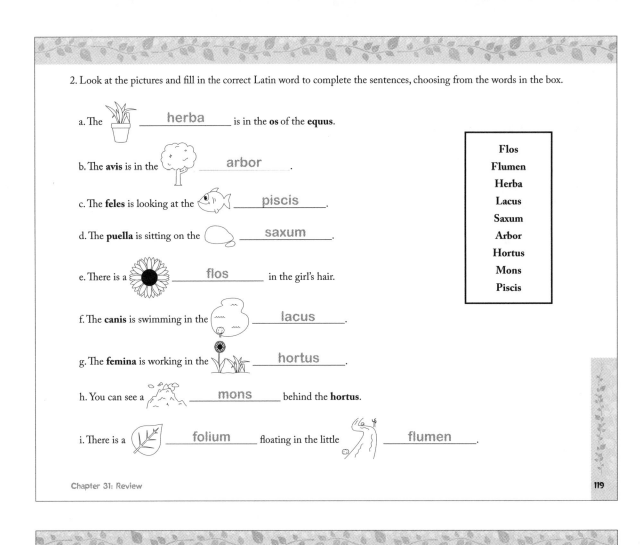

a. The _____ herba _____ is in the **os** of the **equus**.

b. The **avis** is in the _____ arbor _____.

c. The **feles** is looking at the _____ piscis _____.

d. The **puella** is sitting on the _____ saxum _____.

e. There is a _____ flos _____ in the girl's hair.

f. The **canis** is swimming in the _____ lacus _____.

g. The **femina** is working in the _____ hortus _____.

h. You can see a _____ mons _____ behind the **hortus**.

i. There is a _____ folium _____ floating in the little _____ flumen _____.

Flos
Flumen
Herba
Lacus
Saxum
Arbor
Hortus
Mons
Piscis

3. What do you think you would see if you took a hike in the **silva**? Draw a picture with three things that you can name in Latin.

(Answers will vary.)
Suggestions:
arbor (tree)
saxum (rock)
ursa (bear)
folium (leaf)
herba (plant)

4. Draw a line from each item to the place where you would see normally see it—water or dry ground.

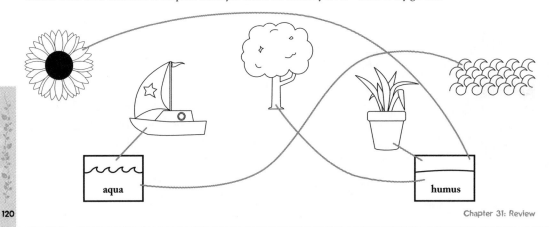

aqua

humus

Chapter-by-Chapter Glossary — Appendix A

Chapter 1: Greeting Words
1. **salve** — hello
2. **vale** — good-bye
3. **discipuli** — students
4. **magister/magistra** — teacher

Chapter 2: Making Friends
1. **Quid est tuum praenomen?** — What is your name?
2. **Meum praenomen est…** — My name is...

Chapter 3: How Are You?
1. **Quid agis?** — How are you?
2. **sum** — I am
3. **bene** — well/fine
4. **optime** — great
5. **pessime** — terrible

Chapter 5: Family Members
1. **pater** — father
2. **mater** — mother
3. **soror** — sister
4. **frater** — brother

Chapter 6: People
1. **puella** — girl
2. **puer** — boy
3. **vir** — man
4. **femina** — woman

Chapter 7: Classroom Items
1. **mensa** — table
2. **sella** — chair
3. **stylus** — pencil
4. **liber** — book

Chapter 8: Household Items
1. **casa** — house
2. **porta** — door
3. **murus** — wall
4. **fenestra** — window

Chapter 10: Classroom Commands
1. **sede** — sit
   sedete — sit (more than 1 person)
2. **surge** — rise/stand up
   surgite — rise/stand up (more than 1 person)
3. **scribe** — write
   scribite — write (more than 1 person)
4. **repete** — repeat
   repetite — repeat (more than 1 person)

Be sure to test your skills in the End-of-Year Crossword on page 141!

Chapter 11: More Classroom Commands
1. **audi** — listen
   audite — listen (more than 1 person)
2. **tace** — be quiet
   tacete — be quiet (more than 1 person)
3. **aperi librum** — open the book
   aperite libros — open the books (more than 1 person)
4. **attole manum** — raise your hand
   attolite manus — raise your hands (more than 1 person)

Chapter 12: Manners
1. **amabo te** — please
2. **tibi gratias ago** — thank you
3. **ignosce mihi** — excuse me

Chapter 14: Pets
1. **canis** — dog
2. **feles** — cat
3. **equus** — horse
4. **piscis** — fish

Chapter 15: Animals
1. **leo** — lion
2. **avis** — bird
3. **ursa** — bear
4. **elephantus** — elephant

Chapter 16: Christmas Words
1. **angelus** — angel
2. **pastor** — shepherd
3. **agnus** — lamb
4. **stella** — star
5. **infans** — baby

Chapter 17: More Christmas Words
1. **cano** — I sing
2. **laudo** — I praise
3. **do** — I give
4. **donum** — gift

Chapter 19: The Body
1. **manus** — hand
2. **pes** — foot
3. **caput** — head
4. **corpus** — body

Chapter 20: The Face
1. **auris** — ear
2. **nares** — nose
3. **oculus** — eye
4. **os** — mouth

Chapter 21: Food Words

1.	cibus	food
2.	aqua	water
3.	cena	dinner
4.	edo	I eat
5.	bibo	I drink

Chapter 22: More Food Words

1.	panis	bread
2.	fructus	fruit
3.	lac	milk
4.	crustulum	cookie
5.	pullus	chicken

Chapter 24: Weather

1.	nix	snow
2.	imber	rain
3.	ventus	wind
4.	nimbus	cloud
5.	arcus	rainbow

Chapter 25: The Seasons

1.	hiems	winter
2.	ver	spring
3.	autumnus	fall
4.	aestas	summer

Chapter 26: The Sky

1.	caelum	sky
2.	luna	moon
3.	stella	star
4.	sol	sun

Chapter 28: Water Words

1.	mare	sea
2.	unda	wave
3.	lacus	lake
4.	flumen	river
5.	navis	ship/boat

Chapter 29: Gardening

1.	flos	flower
2.	herba	plant
3.	hortus	garden
4.	folium	leaf
5.	humus	ground/dirt

Chapter 30: Playing Outdoors

1.	mons	mountain
2.	arbor	tree
3.	saxum	rock
4.	collis	hill
5.	silva	forest

Appendix B   Alphabetical Glossary

aestas	summer
agnus	lamb
amabo te	please
angelus	angel
aperi librum	open the book
aperite libros	open the books (more than 1 person)
aqua	water
arbor	tree
arcus	rainbow
attole manum	raise your hand
attolite manus	raise your hands (more than 1 person)
audi	listen
audite	listen (more than 1 person)
auris	ear
autumnus	fall
avis	bird
bene	well/fine
bibo	I drink
caelum	sky
canis	dog
cano	I sing
caput	head
casa	house
cena	dinner
cibus	food
collis	hill
corpus	body
crustulum	cookie
discipuli	students
do	I give
donum	gift
edo	I eat
elephantus	elephant
equus	horse
feles	cat
femina	woman
fenestra	window
flos	flower
flumen	river
folium	leaf
frater	brother
fructus	fruit
herba	plant
hiems	winter

hortus	garden	nimbus	cloud
humus	ground/dirt	nix	snow
ignosce mihi	excuse me	oculus	eye
imber	rain	optime	great
infans	baby	os	mouth
iratus	angry	panis	bread
lac	milk	pastor	shepherd
lacus	lake	pater	father
laudo	I praise	pes	foot
leo	lion	pessime	terrible
liber	book	piscis	fish
luna	moon	porta	door
magister/magistra	teacher	puella	girl
manus	hand	puer	boy
mare	sea	pullus	chicken
mater	mother	Quid agis?	How are you?
mensa	table	Quid est tuum praenomen?	What is your name?
Meum praenomen est...	My name is...	repete	repeat
mons	mountain	repetite	repeat (more than 1 person)
murus	wall	salve	hello
nares	nose	saxum	rock
navis	ship/boat	scribe	write

scribite	write (more than 1 person)
sede	sit
sedete	sit (more than 1 person)
sella	chair
silva	forest
sol	sun
soror	sister
stella	star
stylus	pencil
sum	I am
surge	rise/stand up
surgite	rise/stand up (more than 1 person)
tace	be quiet
tacete	be quiet (more than 1 person)
tibi gratias ago	thank you
unda	wave
tristis	sad
ursa	bear
vale	good-bye
ventus	wind
ver	spring
vir	man

Looking for more practice?

Look no further! Pages 69–110 contain activities for each chapter in *Song School Latin Book 1*. These are great resources for students who need more practice, have extra time, learn better through games and activities, or simply enjoy Latin. There is one activity page for each chapter, two pages for the review chapters, and a four-page end-of-book review. You can find the answers to each activity in the answer section that starts on page 111.

If you purchased the *Song School Latin Book 1* streaming video from CAP, be sure to check out the free My Library bonus content for more practice activities for your students!

Permission to photocopy the *Song School Latin Book 1* activities (pages 69–110) is granted as long as copies are not used for resale, for use with more than one classroom of students, or for reworking into another game.

©2009 Classical Academic Press • All rights reserved.

```
C  U  H  G  D  M  F  L  U  V
T  B  X  D  S  A  L  V  E  I
Y  V  U  I  B  G  J  H  R  U
I  O  C  S  A  I  O  C  L  S
D  R  X  C  V  S  M  B  V  A
M  A  G  I  S  T  E  R  M  T
O  R  E  P  A  R  L  A  N  L
V  N  I  U  V  A  L  E  G  V
A  G  K  L  R  U  P  B  R  T
L  A  M  I  S  T  E  F  T  E
```

1. Translate the English words below into Latin and then find the Latin words in the word search!

    a. hello   _____

    b. good-bye   _____

    c. student   _____

    d. teacher   _____

                Double Points if you can find both words for teacher!

2. What is the one English letter that does not exist in the Latin alphabet? _____ 69

CHAPTER 2: Making Friends

1. Each *discipuli* is saying a Latin vowel sound! In the blank, write the letter that the *discipuli* is saying.

2. In Latin, ask the monkey what his name is:

_____

3. Now, tell the monkey your name!

_____

1. Draw a face that shows how each person feels.

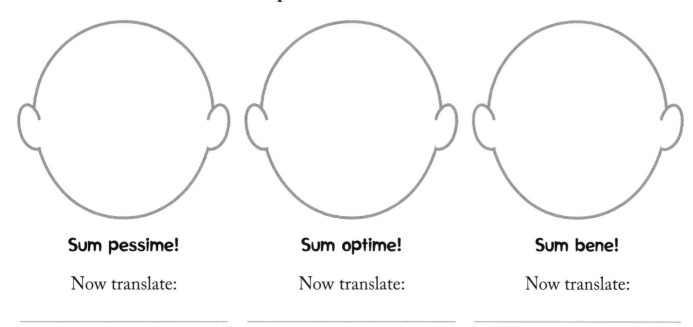

Sum pessime!

Now translate:

_____

Sum optime!

Now translate:

_____

Sum bene!

Now translate:

_____

2. Draw a line from the Latin word or phrase to the correct English word or phrase.

discipuli   sum   discipula   Quid agis?   discipulus

I am

students

a boy student

a girl student

How are you?

1. Translate the English words into Latin and fill in the crossword puzzle!

Across
3. I am
4. terrible
7. students
9. good-bye
10. How are you?
11. female teacher
12. well/fine

Down
1. boy student
2. girl student
5. hello
6. male teacher
8. great

(Continued on next page!)

2. The chapter two phrases got mixed up! See if you can put them back together by using the word bank below.

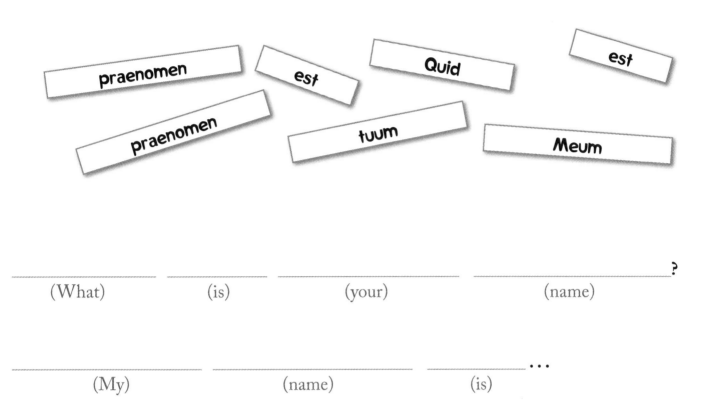

praenomen

est

Quid

est

praenomen

tuum

Meum

_____ _____ _____ _____?
(What)   (is)   (your)   (name)

_____ _____ _____...
(My)   (name)   (is)

Create a family tree! Draw the faces of your family and label each one with the correct Latin word (see the word bank below). Add more faces if you need to!

Pater _____

Mater _____

Frater _____

Soror _____

Bonus points!
See if you can translate the Latin words in the word bank.

```
F  P  U  E  L  L  A  O  P  A
R  A  R  I  G  Z  T  V  X  H
V  T  U  G  S  A  E  F  I  O
X  E  F  D  Y  O  B  Q  P  K
P  R  E  K  L  D  R  L  U  Y
Q  A  M  P  L  N  D  O  E  M
X  D  I  F  A  V  C  X  R  A
Y  K  N  L  H  I  G  E  A  T
F  R  A  T  E  R  D  L  B  E
P  Z  N  I  L  B  V  M  N  R
```

1. **Translate the English words below into Latin and then find the Latin words in the word search!**

    a. boy   _____

    b. woman   _____

    c. girl   _____

    d. man   _____

    Double Points if you can find: *pater*, *mater*, *frater*, and *soror*!
    Make sure you look for diagonals!

2. **What kind of word names a person, place, or thing?** _____

1. **Translate the Latin words!**

    a. sella   _____   c. liber   _____

    b. mensa   _____   d. stylus   _____

2. **In the picture frame below, draw a classroom that includes a *sella*, a *mensa*, a *liber*, and a *stylus*.**

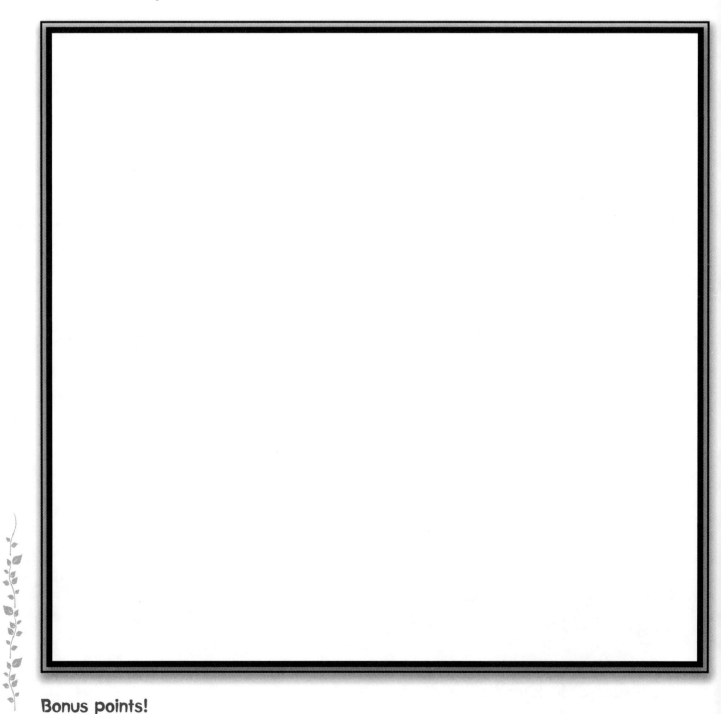

Bonus points!

See if you can include *discipuli* and a *magister* or *magistra* in your drawing.

Answer the questions by drawing a line to the correct object. Then, write the Latin word for each object.

1. To enter a room, you usually go through what?

2. When sitting down for dinner, you usually sit on what?

3. What do you use to write with?

4. What do you live in?

5. If you are inside and want to look outside, what can you look through?

6. What do you read at the library?

7. What is on the outside of your house that helps to hold up the roof?

8. When you eat dinner, on what do you place your food?

_____
(house)

_____
(pencil)

_____
(chair)

_____
(wall)

_____
(door)

_____
(table)

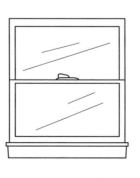

_____
(window)

_____
(book)

1. Translate the English words into Latin and fill in the crossword puzzle!

Across

4. window
6. wall
8. girl
10. chair
11. mother
13. door
14. pencil

Down

1. brother
2. woman
3. man
5. sister
6. table
7. boy
8. father
9. book
12. house

2. From what Latin word did the word "library" come? _____
(Hint: it's in the crossword puzzle!)

(Continued on next page!)

3. In the room below, draw some of the objects from this chapter and label them with their Latin names. Use the pictures below to help you. One has already been done for you.

murus

1. Match each command to the child who is doing the correct action.

a. scribe

b. repete

c. surge

d. sede

VIR

VIR

2. Tell a crowd!

a. Tell more than one person to repeat: _____

b. Tell more than one person to stand: _____

c. Tell more than one person to write: _____

d. Tell more than one person to sit: _____

```
Q  T  R  Y  I  O  P  S  N  G
K  A  U  D  I  L  A  C  X  R
X  C  J  R  P  S  U  R  G  E
F  E  X  E  K  X  D  I  S  P
S  T  F  P  J  N  I  B  U  E
E  E  D  E  M  L  T  E  R  T
D  P  D  T  A  C  E  K  G  I
E  M  K  E  F  P  D  V  I  T
T  L  S  C  R  I  B  I  T  E
E  V  N  J  O  G  M  X  E  D
```

1. **Translate the English words below into Latin and then find the Latin words in the word search!**

    a. listen   _____

    b. listen (plural)   _____

    c. be quiet   _____

    d. be quiet (plural)   _____

    Double Points if you can find: *sede, sedete, scribe, scribite, surge, surgite, repete,* and *repetite*!
Make sure you look for diagonals!

2. **From what Latin word does the word "auditorium" come?** _____   81

1. The chapter twelve phrases got mixed up! See if you can put them back together by using the word bank below.

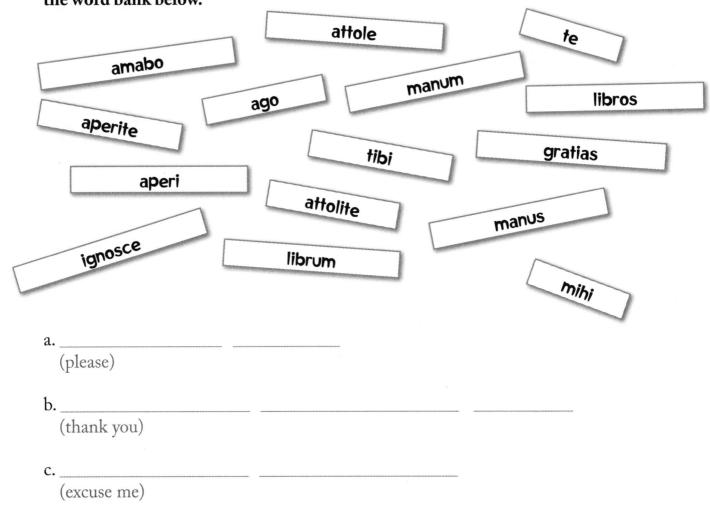

attole

te

amabo

manum

ago

libros

aperite

tibi

gratias

aperi

attolite

manus

ignosce

librum

mihi

a. _____ _____
   (please)

b. _____ _____ _____
   (thank you)

c. _____ _____
   (excuse me)

2. Can you put together the phrases from chapter eleven too?
   (Keep using the above word bank)

a. _____ _____
   (open the book—to one person)

b. _____ _____
   (open the book—to more than one person)

c. _____ _____
   (raise your hand—to one person)

d. _____ _____
   (raise your hand—to more than one person)

1. Translate the English words into Latin and fill in the crossword puzzle!

Across

1. rise/stand up
5. sit
6. write (plural)
8. sit (plural)
10. please
11. be quiet
12. repeat

Down

2. repeat (plural)
3. write
4. listen
7. excuse me
8. rise/stand up (plural)
9. be quiet (plural)
10. listen (plural)

VIR

VIR

2. The English word "scribble" comes from what Latin word? _____
   Now scribble in the box below!

(Continued on next page!)

3. Translate the English into Latin by writing one Latin letter in each box.

a. Raise your hand (plural):

1

b. Open the book:

6

c. Thank you:

3

d. Open the book (plural):

2   4

e. Raise your hand:

5

4. Discover how well you did! In the activity above, find the numbers and write the letter in the corresponding blank below.

____ ____ ____ ____ ____ ____!
1   2   3   4   5   6

1. Draw a picture of each animal!

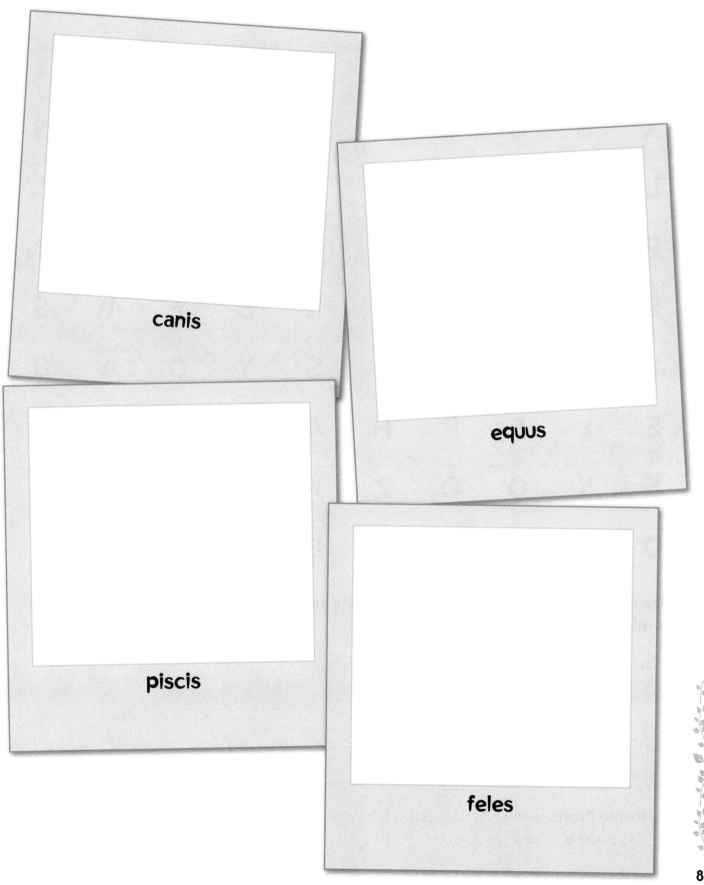

canis

equus

piscis

feles

```
R  A  L  T  P  N  Q  U  K  P
Q  D  E  N  J  S  C  C  A  I
X  U  O  Q  M  B  A  O  Z  S
L  R  N  V  U  R  N  V  K  C
F  P  I  S  E  U  I  Y  I  I
E  A  V  I  A  R  S  F  M  S
L  F  O  B  R  S  Y  O  A  J
E  L  E  P  H  A  N  T  U  S
S  K  Q  O  Z  F  E  H  N  G
D  F  U  N  V  E  C  I  S  L
```

1. **Translate the English words below into Latin and then find the Latin words in the word search!**

    a. lion   _____

    b. bear   _____

    c. elephant   _____

    d. bird   _____

Double Points if you can find: *canis*, *feles*, *equus*, and *piscis*!
Make sure you look for diagonals!

2. **How do you say "beware of the dog" in Latin?** _____

1. On the scene below, draw images of all the words from this chapter. Then, label each image with its Latin word. Use the word bank to help you. The first one is done for you.

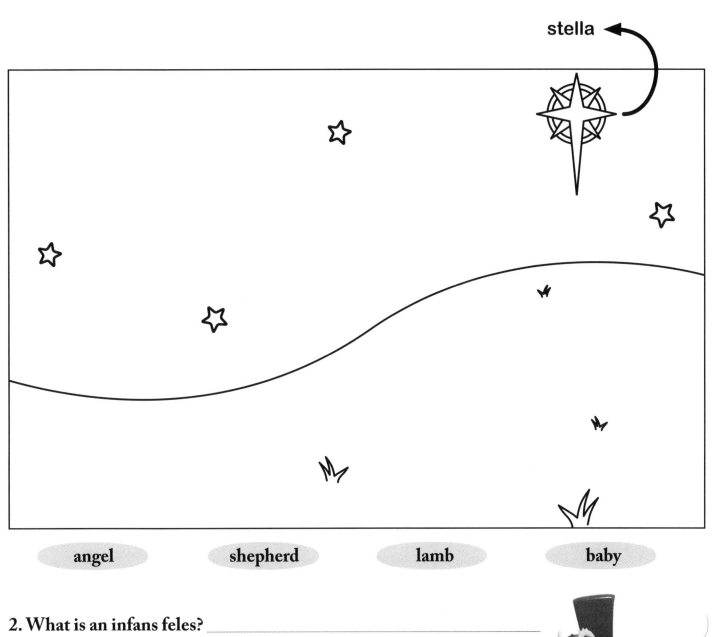

stella

| angel | shepherd | lamb | baby |

2. What is an infans feles? _____

3. How would you say "rare bird" in Latin?

_____

1. Translate the English into Latin then match the word to the correct picture!

a. I give   _____

b. I praise   _____

c. gift   _____

d. I sing   _____

2. The first line of Vergil's book has become mixed up! Can you put it back together using the word bank below?

virumque	cano	arma

" _____ _____ _____ ."

3. In Vergil's quote, do you see the Latin word for "I sing"? Draw a circle around the word and then write it here:

_____

4. Look again at Vergil's quote. Do you see the word for "man"? Look very closely; it is hidden inside a word! When you find it, draw a box around it and write it here:

_____

1. Translate the English words to Latin and fill in the crossword puzzle! Then color the page!

Across

3. gift
5. angel
8. lamb
10. fish
12. lion
13. dog
14. horse
17. I sing

Down

1. baby
2. bear
4. shepherd
6. elephant
7. bird
9. cat
11. I give
15. star
16. I praise

(Continued on next page!)

2. **Do you remember the difference between nouns and verbs? Nouns are things you can touch and verbs are action words! Look at the words below. Circle all the nouns, and underline all the verbs.**

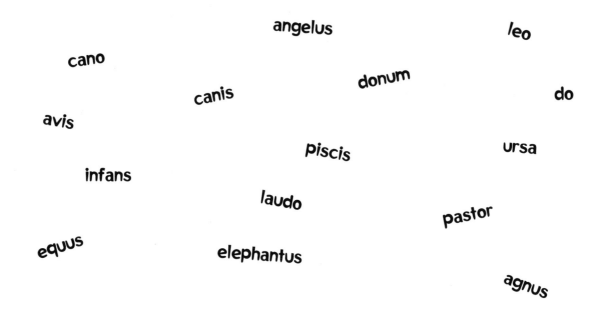

angelus   leo

cano

canis   donum   do

avis

piscis   ursa

infans

laudo

pastor

equus   elephantus

agnus

3. **What is the special ending on the end of these verbs that means "I"?** _____

4. **Most of the words you've learned thus far are (circle one):**   nouns   verbs

5. **Answer the questions by drawing a line to the correct word:**

   a. What do you see in the night sky?   do

   b. What animal makes nests in trees?   canis

   c. What were you when you were born?   stella

   d. What animals says "woof, woof!"   feles

   e. What do you do with a *donum*?   avis

   f. From what animal do we get wool?   cano

   g. Who takes care of flocks?   infans

   h. What do you do with a song?   agnus

   i. What animal says "meow!"   pastor

1. Translate the English word into Latin. Then draw a line to the correct part of the monkey!

a. Body _____

b. Foot _____

c. Head _____

d. Hand _____

2. How do you say "the voice of the people" in Latin? _____

3. Many English words come from Latin words! Look at the list of English words on the left and try to match them up with the correct Latin words on the right. Here's a hint: if the words look similar, they are probably related!

a. Manuscript *(something written by hand)*   Corpus

b. Pedestrian *(someone who is on foot)*   Manus

c. Captain *(the head person in charge of a boat)*   Liber

d. Library *(a place that has lots of books)*   Pes

e. Corps *(the body of the military; the officers)*   Audi

f. Audience *(a group of people who listen)*   Caput

g. Donation *(a gift)*   Infans

h. Constellation *(a grouping of stars)*   Donum

i. Infant *(a small baby)*   Feles

j. Feline *(belonging to the cat family)*   Stella

Using the picture and instructions below, help us create Sammy the Spy! Check off the boxes after you do each step.

- ☐ 1. Draw two **auris** on his **caput**.
- ☐ 2. Draw sunglasses over his **oculus**.
- ☐ 3. Draw a straight line for his **os**.
- ☐ 4. Draw big boots on his two **pes**.
- ☐ 5. Draw a long coat over his **corpus**.
- ☐ 6. Draw a walking stick in his **manus**.
- ☐ 7. Draw a **nares** on his face.
- ☐ 8. Draw a **stylus** behind one **auris**.
- ☐ 9. Draw a cowboy hat on his **caput**.
- ☐ 10. Draw an **avis** on one **manus**.

```
A  E  R  P  Y  A  Q  U  A  S
D  X  F  T  S  I  F  D  M  G
L  C  D  X  A  L  J  T  O  H
J  S  I  Z  I  E  D  V  K  N
I  Y  Q  B  O  M  P  I  N  S
S  D  R  I  U  D  V  U  Q  R
A  F  U  B  T  S  Y  C  A  D
I  E  D  O  G  P  O  E  S  F
P  T  S  F  E  S  Z  N  R  L
H  U  Q  Y  J  I  X  A  K  N
```

1. **Translate the English words below into Latin and then find the Latin words in the word search!**

   a. food   _____

   b. dinner   _____

   c. I eat   _____

   d. water   _____

   e. I drink   _____

2. **How many of the above words are verbs?** _____

Translate the following Latin words, then draw the objects in the refrigerator!

☐ 1. A box of **crustulum** _____

☐ 2. A loaf of **panis** _____

☐ 3. A gallon of **lac** _____

☐ 4. **Pullus** nuggets _____

☐ 5. A basket of **fructus** _____

☐ 6. A bottle of **aqua** _____

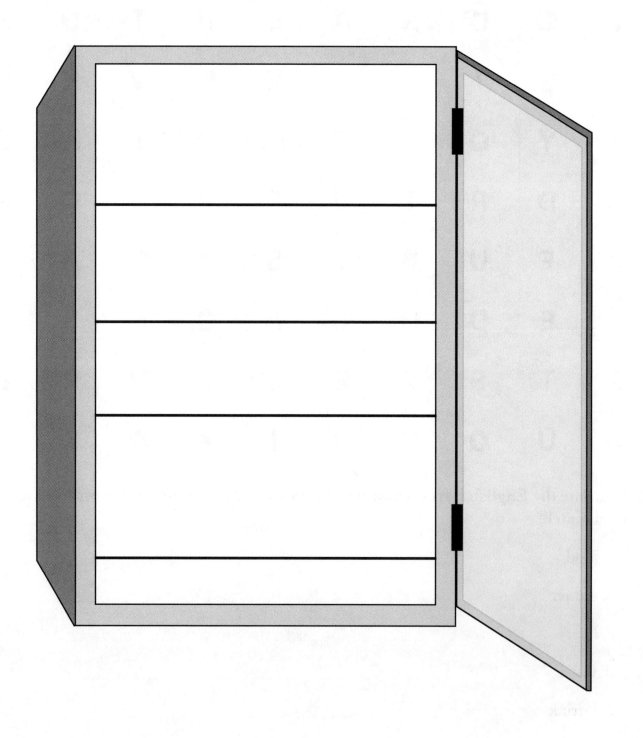

1. Translate the English words to Latin and fill in the crossword puzzle! Then color the page!

Across
3. bread
6. dinner
8. I drink
10. chicken
11. ear
13. hand
14. I eat
16. body
17. milk
18. mouth

Down
1. fruit
2. foot
4. nose
5. food
7. water
9. cookie
12. head
15. eye

(Continued on next page!)

2. What does *et cetera* mean? _____

3. The English word "pantry" comes from which Latin word? (circle one)

lac   panis   cibus

4. The English word "aquarium" comes from which Latin word? (circle one)

aqua   bibo   crustulum

5. Answer the questions by drawing a line to the correct word:

a. If you are thirsty, what do you do?   fructus

b. What part of your body do you use to think?   auris

c. What liquid do you find in rivers?   bibo

d. Apples and oranges are both what kind of *cibus*?   os

e. What part of your body do you use to hear?   pes

f. When you want to speak or eat, what do you use? aqua

g. What liquid comes from cows?   caput

h. What part of your body do you use to see?   oculus

i. What part of your body do you use to walk?   lac

6. **Color and label the images below!**

  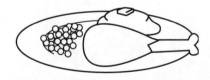

_____   _____   _____

Read the weather report for each day, then draw a picture of that day's weather in the correct circle. Then, label each image with its Latin word.

Monday: Heavy *imber* and dark *nimbus* all day long.

Tuesday: Strong *ventus* in the morning.

Wednesday: Many *nimbus* with slight chance of *nix*.

Thursday: Light *imber*, probably resulting in an *arcus* in the afternoon.

Friday: Sunshine and a few light, fluffy *nimbus*.

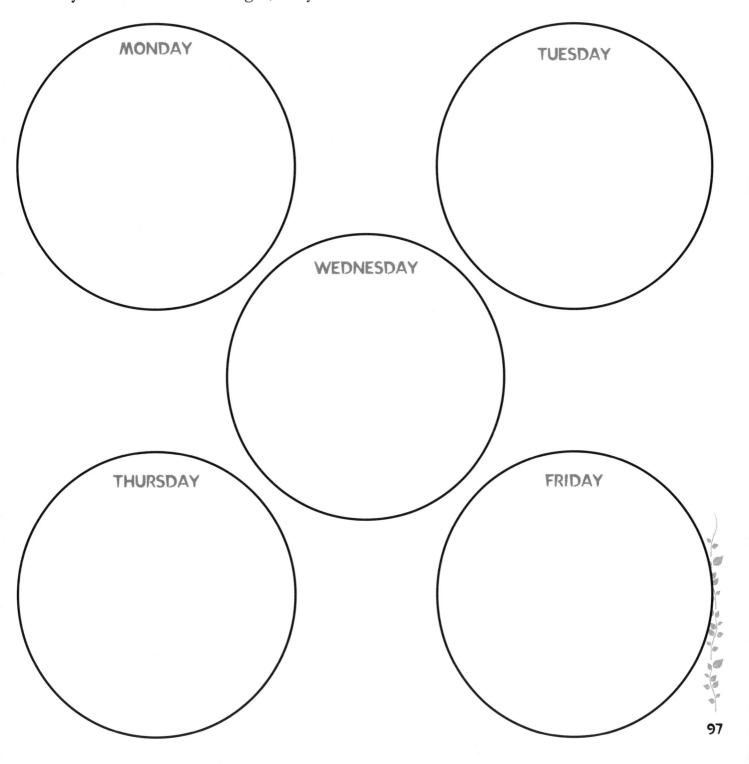

1. **Read the sentence about the season, then draw a line from the sentence to the season, and from the season to the weather!**

a. During *hiems*, *nix* makes the
ground and trees white.

summer

b. In *autumnus*, the *ventus* blows
the orange and gold leaves.

spring

c. During *aestas* the sky is full
of sun and light, fluffy *nimbus*.

winter

d. In *ver*, *imber* falls, and you
might see an *arcus*.

fall

2. **This week's Latin saying has become scrambled! Can you put the letters in the right order? Hint: make sure you work slowly!**

_____ _____ _____ _____ _____ _____

_____ _____ _____

3. **Now translate the saying:** _____

1. **Fill up the night *caelum* with lots of *stella* and then add a *luna*. On the day side, draw a big, bright *sol*.**

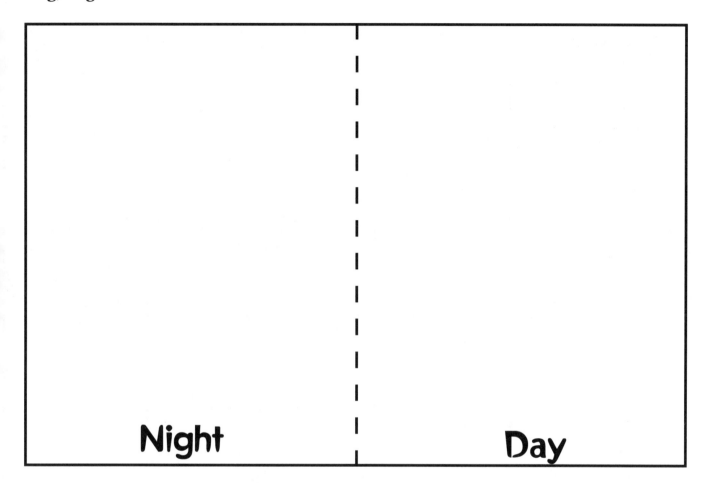

Night   Day

2. **This week's Latin saying is *e pluribus unum*. Can you translate each part below?**

e pluribus	=	_____
unum	=	_____

3. **Many English words come from Latin words! Look at the list of English words on the left and try to match them up with the correct Latin words on the right. Here's a hint: if the words look similar, they are probably related!**

a. Lunar *(having to do with the <u>moon</u>)*

b. Arc *(a curve like that of a <u>rainbow</u>)*

c. Autumn *(another name for the <u>fall</u> season)*

d. Pantry *(a place where people might keep <u>bread</u>)*

Arcus

Autumnus

Luna

Panis

1. Translate the English words to Latin and fill in the crossword puzzle! Then color the page!

Across
1. spring
3. snow
4. sky
7. fall
10. star
12. cloud

Down
1. wind
2. moon
5. summer
6. rain
8. winter
9. sun
11. rainbow

2. Translate the English into the correct Latin saying.

a. Make haste slowly:

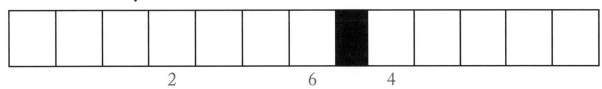

b. Out of many, one:

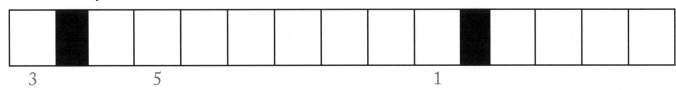

3. Discover how well you did! In the activity above find the numbers and write the letter in the corresponding blank below.

You're a ____ ____ ____ ____ ____ ____!
                1   2   3   4   5   6

4. Answer the questions by drawing a line to the correct word:

a. The night sky contains many *stella* and one _____.

b. What is cold, white and falls from the sky in winter?

c. What blows the leaves off the trees?

d. During which season is the weather hot and sunny?

e. What season is cold and might have *nix*?

f. What falls in drops from the *caelum*?

g. On a sunny day, you know that the _____ is shining.

h. What are the white fluffy objects in the *caelum*?

i. During which season do flowers start to bloom?

j. During which season do leaves turn yellow, orange, and red?

k. What is the colorful arc you might see after the *imber*?

aestas

hiems

imber

luna

nix

ventus

ver

sol

nimbus

arcus

autumnus

```
A  S  C  F  N  A  V  I  S  M
R  O  U  E  K  L  N  C  T  I
G  L  U  N  A  D  J  P  E  U
M  E  B  X  D  L  F  M  L  B
Q  T  C  G  I  A  Y  A  L  X
D  L  A  N  O  C  H  R  A  T
I  H  E  F  L  U  M  E  N  G
J  R  L  O  B  S  J  Z  U  M
A  V  U  F  P  I  S  C  I  S
Z  C  M  N  H  E  L  X  D  Y
```

Translate the English words below into Latin and then find the Latin words in the word search!

a. lake _____

b. river _____

c. ship/boat _____

d. sea _____

e. wave _____

Double Points if you can find: *caelum*, *luna*, *stella*, *sol*, and *piscis*!
Make sure you look for diagonals!

Time to draw!

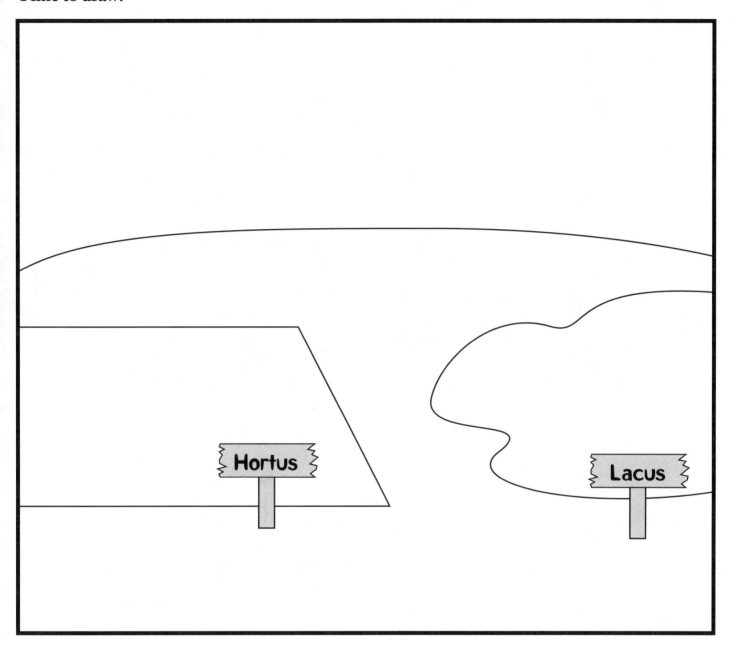

Follow the instructions and fill in the picture!
1. Draw some bumpy *humus* in the *hortus*.
2. Draw a few rows of *herba* in the *hortus*.
3. Put a few *flos* on some of the *herba*.
4. In the *caelum*, draw a strong *ventus* blowing around three *folium*.
5. Put a few *unda* in the *lacus*.
6. On one of the *unda*, draw a small *navis*.
7. Above another *unda*, draw a jumping *piscis*.
8. Put a white, fluffy *nimbus* in the *caelum*.
9. Draw the *sol* peeking out behind the *nimbus*.
10. Draw a colorful *pullus* scratching the ground in front of the *hortus*.

Label each picture with its Latin name!

(tree)

(mountain)

(rock)

(forest)

(hill)

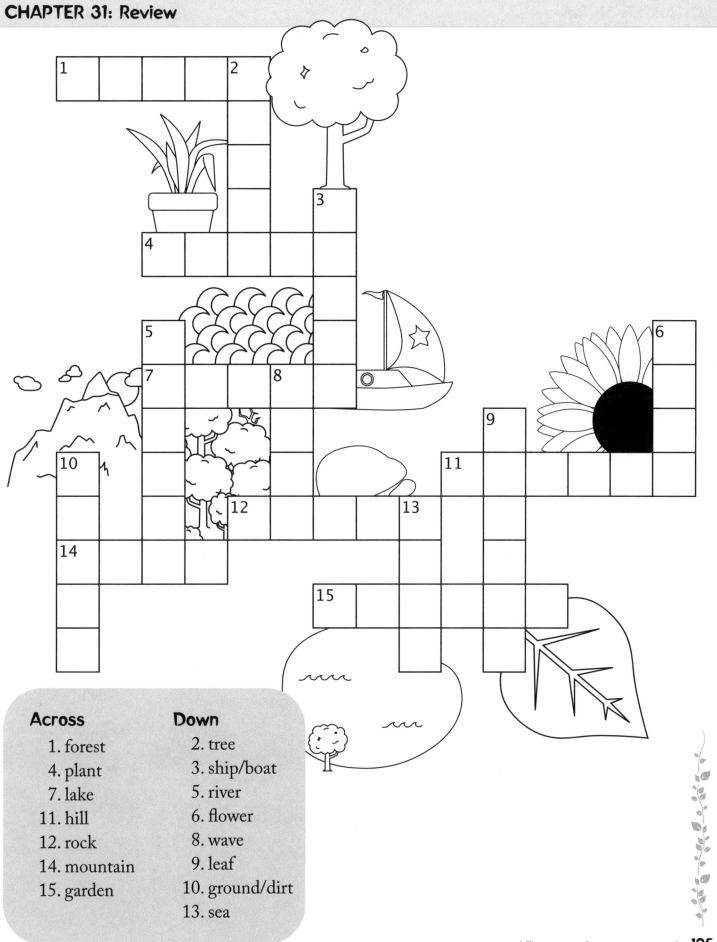

Across
1. forest
4. plant
7. lake
11. hill
12. rock
14. mountain
15. garden

Down
2. tree
3. ship/boat
5. river
6. flower
8. wave
9. leaf
10. ground/dirt
13. sea

(Continued on next page!)

2. **The Latin phrases got scrambled! Help unscramble the phrases by answering the questions using the scrambled letters as a word bank.**

a. If you spill *aqua* on your *feles*, how would you tell her it's your fault in Latin?

_____ _____ _____ _____ _____ _____ _____ _____!

b. If a *puer* has recently been on a boat, how would he say he's glad to back on "solid ground"?

_____ _____ _____ _____ _____

_____ _____ _____ _____ _____

3. **Many English words come from Latin words! Look at the list of English words on the left and try to match them up with the correct Latin words on the right. Here's a hint: if the words look similar, they are probably related!**

a. Navy *(a part of the military with many ships)*

b. Herb *(a type of plant)*

c. Foliage *(the leaves of a plant)*

d. Humble *(to be lowly, as if on the ground)*

e. Undulation *(the motion of the waves)*

f. Sylvan *(a wooded area, like a forest)*

g. Horticulture *(the science of growing a garden)*

h. Submarine *(a machine that travels under the sea)*

Herba

Unda

Navis

Humus

Mare

Silva

Folium

Hortus

1. Label the numbered objects by writing their Latin name in the corresponding blank below. Then color the picture!

1. _____   6. _____   11. _____

2. _____   7. _____   12. _____

3. _____   8. _____   13. _____

4. _____   9. _____   14. _____

5. _____   10. _____   15. _____

(Continued on next page!)

2. Draw a picture to match each of the sentences.

An *equus* jumping over the *luna*.

A *leo* with big *auris* and a small *nares*.

A *pastor* and an *agnus*, sitting under an *arcus*.

A *feles* reading a *liber* and sitting in a *fenestra*.

A *canis* sitting on a *sella*.

An *elephantus* next to a *pullus*.

(Continued on next page!)

```
B  H  C  M  U  R  U  S  O  S
D  P  U  E  L  L  A  E  P  C
I  Q  G  N  A  H  Z  D  T  R
S  M  K  S  C  S  P  E  I  I
C  A  S  A  X  T  A  U  M  B
I  T  L  U  B  Y  T  H  E  E
P  E  J  V  A  L  E  L  H  R
U  R  G  I  E  U  R  U  C  Y
L  L  B  R  Q  S  E  L  L  A
I  Z  F  E  M  I  N  A  G  P
```

3. **Translate the English words below into Latin and then find the Latin words in the word search!**

a. hello _____

b. great _____

c. father _____

d. table _____

e. mother _____

f. students _____

g. chair _____

h. good-bye _____

i. girl _____

j. boy _____

Double Points if you can find: *vir, stylus, murus, sede, lac, scribe,* and *femina*!
Make sure you look for diagonals!

(Continued on next page!) **109**

4. Match the Latin word to the correct picture, then color the picture!

Surge

Repete

Porta

Soror

Frater

Magistra

Angelus

Stella

Cano

Donum

Manus

Oculus

Os

Cibus

Edo

Bibo

Panis

Crustulum

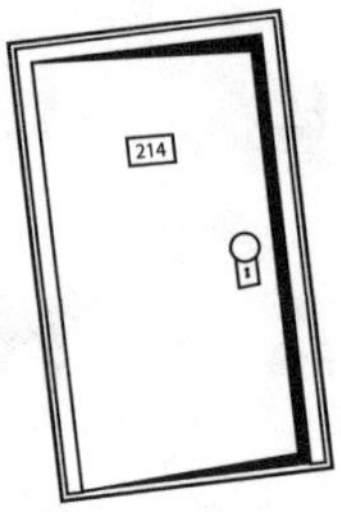

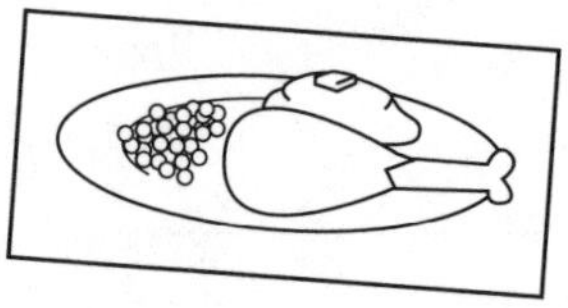

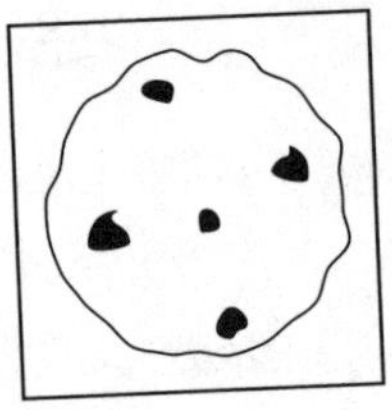

Song School Latin Activity Answers

Pages 111–132 contain the answers for the previous activities. These are most easily viewed if you turn the book 90 degrees clockwise (as if it were a calendar.)

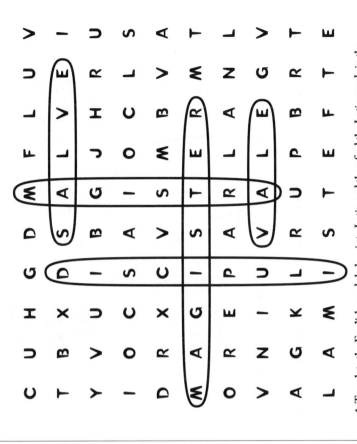

CHAPTER 1: Greeting Words

```
C  U  H  G  D  M  F  L  U  V
T  B  X  D  U  B  J  H  R  U
Y  V  U  I  S  A  O  C  L  S
I  O  C  A  C  V  M  B  V  A
D  R  X  V  S  T  E  R  M  T
M  A  G  I  S  G  I  E  A  N  L
O  R  E  P  A  R  L  A  G  V
V  N  I  U  L  R  U  P  B  R  T
A  G  K  L  R  U  B  T
L  A  M  I  S  T  E  F  T  E
```

1. Translate the English words below into Latin and then find the Latin words in the word search!

   a. hello   **salve**

   b. good-bye   **vale**

   c. student   **discipuli**

   d. teacher   **magister/magistra**

   Double Points if you can find both words for teacher!

2. What is the one English letter that does not exist in the Latin alphabet?   **W**

69

CHAPTER 2: Making Friends

1. Each *discipuli* is saying a Latin vowel sound! In the blank, write the letter that the *discipuli* is saying.

A

I

U

O

E

2. In Latin, ask the monkey what his name is:

Quid est tuum praenomen?

3. Now, tell the monkey your name!

Meum praenomen est . . .

CHAPTER 3: How Are You?

1. Draw a face that shows how each person feels.

Sum pessime!
Now translate:
I am terrible!

Sum optime!
Now translate:
I am great!

Sum bene!
Now translate:
I am well/fine!

2. Draw a line from the Latin word or phrase to the correct English word or phrase.

discipulus — a boy student

Quid agis? — How are you?

discipula — students

sum — a girl student

discipuli — I am

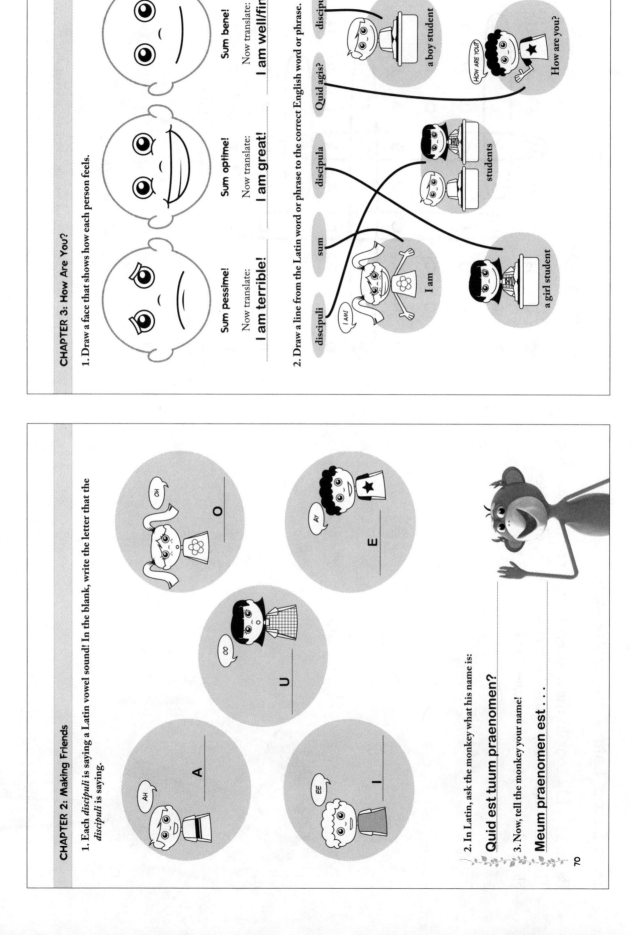

CHAPTER 4: Review

1. Translate the English words into Latin and fill in the crossword puzzle!

Across
3. I am
4. terrible
7. students
9. good-bye
10. How are you?
11. female teacher
12. well/fine

Down
1. boy student
2. girl student
5. hello
6. male teacher
8. great

72

CHAPTER 4: Review

2. The chapter two phrases got mixed up! See if you can put them back together by using the word bank below.

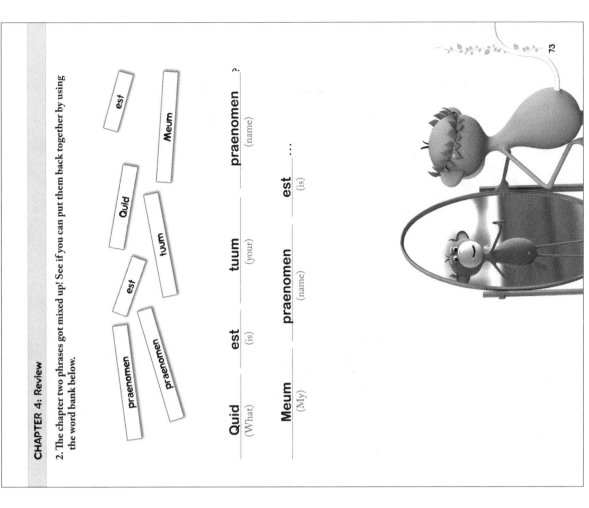

| praenomen | est | Quid | Meum |
| praenomen | tuum | | est |

Quid _____ est _____ tuum _____ praenomen _____ ?
(What)   (is)   (your)   (name)

Meum _____ praenomen _____ est _____ ...
(My)   (name)   (is)

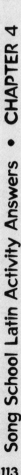

73

Song School Latin Activity Answers • **CHAPTER 4**

113

CHAPTER 5: Family Members

Create a family tree! Draw the faces of your family and label each one with the correct Latin word (see the word bank below). Add more faces if you need to!

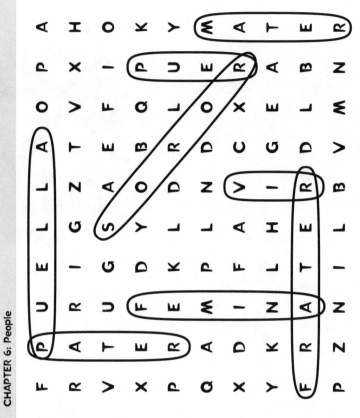

Drawings may vary

Bonus points!
See if you can translate the Latin words in the word bank.

Pater	Father
Mater	Mother
Frater	Brother
Soror	Sister

74

CHAPTER 6: People

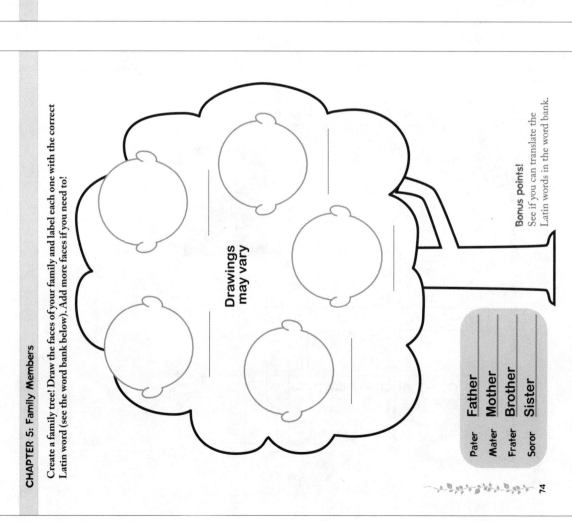

1. Translate the English words below into Latin and then find the Latin words in the word search!

a. boy   **puer**

b. woman   **femina**

c. girl   **puella**

d. man   **vir**

Double Points if you can find: *pater, mater, frater,* and *soror!* Make sure you look for diagonals!

2. What kind of word names a person, place, or thing? _____ **noun**

75

CHAPTER 8: Household Items

Answer the questions by drawing a line to the correct object. Then, write the Latin word for each object.

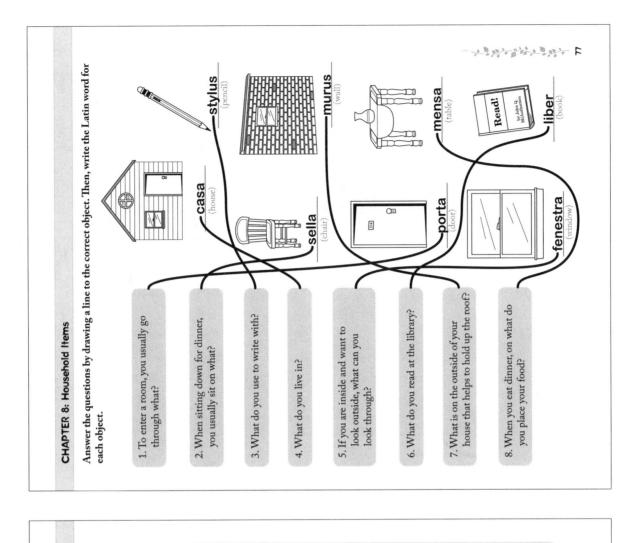

stylus
(pencil)

casa
(house)

sella
(chair)

murus
(wall)

mensa
(table)

porta
(door)

fenestra
(window)

liber
(book)

1. To enter a room, you usually go through what?

2. When sitting down for dinner, you usually sit on what?

3. What do you use to write with?

4. What do you live in?

5. If you are inside and want to look outside, what can you look through?

6. What do you read at the library?

7. What is on the outside of your house that helps to hold up the roof?

8. When you eat dinner, on what do you place your food?

77

CHAPTER 7: Classroom Items

1. Translate the Latin words!

a. sella   **chair**   c. liber   **book**

b. mensa   **table**   d. stylus   **pencil**

2. In the picture frame below, draw a classroom that includes a *sella*, a *mensa*, a *liber*, and a *stylus*.

Drawings will vary.

The translated instructions are: "In the picture frame below, draw a classroom that includes a *chair*, a *table*, a *book*, and a *pencil*.

Bonus points! See if you can include *students* and a *male teacher* or *female teacher* in your drawing."

Bonus points!

See if you can include *discipuli* and a *magister* or *magistra* in your drawing.

76

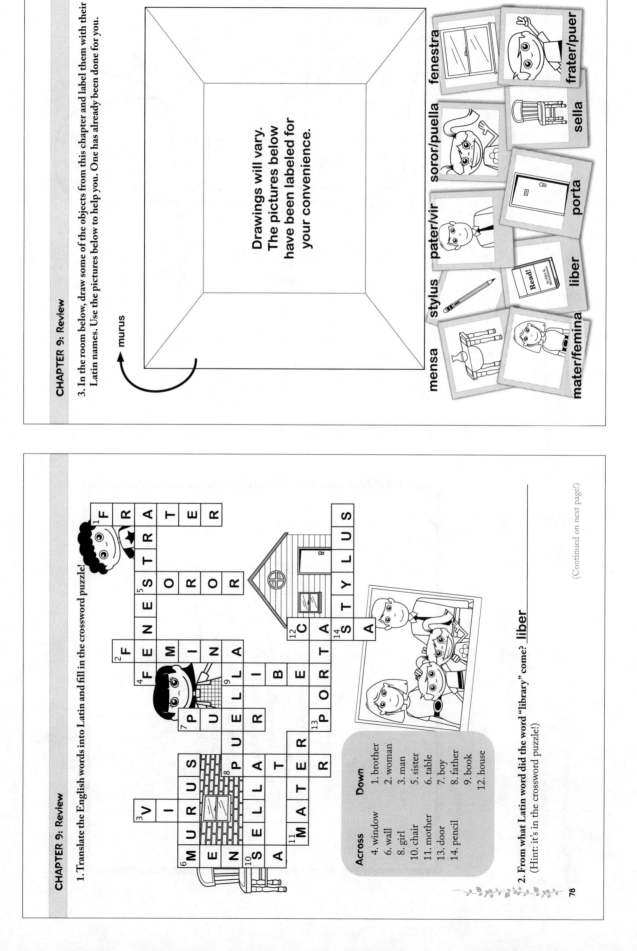

CHAPTER 9: Review

1. Translate the English words into Latin and fill in the crossword puzzle!

Across
4. window
6. wall
8. girl
10. chair
11. mother
13. door
14. pencil

Down
1. brother
2. woman
3. man
5. sister
6. table
7. boy
8. father
9. book
12. house

2. From what Latin word did the word "library" come? liber
(Hint: it's in the crossword puzzle!)

(Continued on next page!)

78

CHAPTER 9: Review

3. In the room below, draw some of the objects from this chapter and label them with their Latin names. Use the pictures below to help you. One has already been done for you.

murus

Drawings will vary.
The pictures below
have been labeled for
your convenience.

fenestra

frater/puer

soror/puella

sella

pater/vir

porta

stylus

liber

mensa

mater/femina

79

CHAPTER 11: More Classroom Commands

Q	R	Y	I	O	P	S	N	G
K	A	U	D	I	L	A	C	X	E
X	C	J	X	K	P	S	U	G	E
F	E	X	F	E	D	I	R	I	P
S	E	D	P	D	M	N	B	E	T
E	D	D	E	M	L	T	A	C	E
D	P	K	E	A	N	I	C	E	K
E	M	F	P	D	T	B	I	V	T	E
T	L	S	C	R	I	B	I	T	E
E	V	N	J	O	G	M	X	E	D

1. Translate the English words below into Latin and then find the Latin words in the word search!

a. listen   __audi__

b. listen (plural)   __audite__

c. be quiet   __tace__

d. be quiet (plural)   __tacete__

Double Points if you can find: *sede, sedete, scribe, scribite, surge, surgite, repete,* and *repetite!* Make sure you look for diagonals!

2. From what Latin word does the word "auditorium" come? __audi__

81

CHAPTER 10: Classroom Commands

1. Match each command to the child who is doing the correct action.

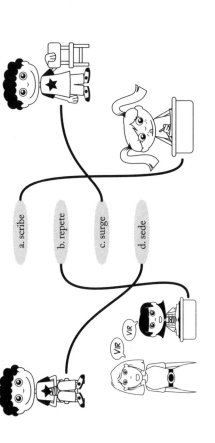

a. scribe

b. repete

c. surge

d. sede

2. Tell a crowd!

a. Tell more than one person to repeat: __Repetite!__

b. Tell more than one person to stand: __Surgite!__

c. Tell more than one person to write: __Scribite!__

d. Tell more than one person to sit: __Sedete!__

Song School Latin Activity Answers • CHAPTERS 10–11

117

CHAPTER 12: Manners

1. The chapter twelve phrases got mixed up! See if you can put them back together by using the word bank below.

Word bank: te, libros, gratias, manus, mihi, attole, manum, tibi, attolite, librum, amabo, aperite, ago, aperi, ignosce

a. **amabo** **te**
   (please)

b. **tibi** **gratias** **ago**
   (thank you)

c. **ignosce** **mihi**
   (excuse me)

2. Can you put together the phrases from chapter eleven too? (Keep using the above word bank)

a. **aperi** **librum**
   (open the book—to one person)

b. **aperite** **libros**
   (open the book—to more than one person)

c. **attole** **manum**
   (raise your hand—to one person)

d. **attolite** **manus**
   (raise your hand—to more than one person)

CHAPTER 13: Review

1. Translate the English words into Latin and fill in the crossword puzzle!

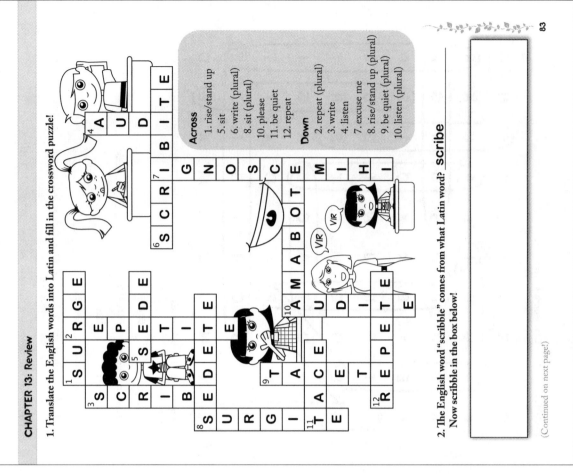

Across
1. rise/stand up
5. sit
6. write (plural)
8. sit (plural)
10. please
11. be quiet
12. repeat

Down
2. repeat (plural)
3. write
4. listen
7. excuse me
8. rise/stand up (plural)
9. be quiet (plural)
10. listen (plural)

2. The English word "scribble" comes from what Latin word? **scribe**
Now scribble in the box below!

(Continued on next page!)

1. Draw a picture of each animal!

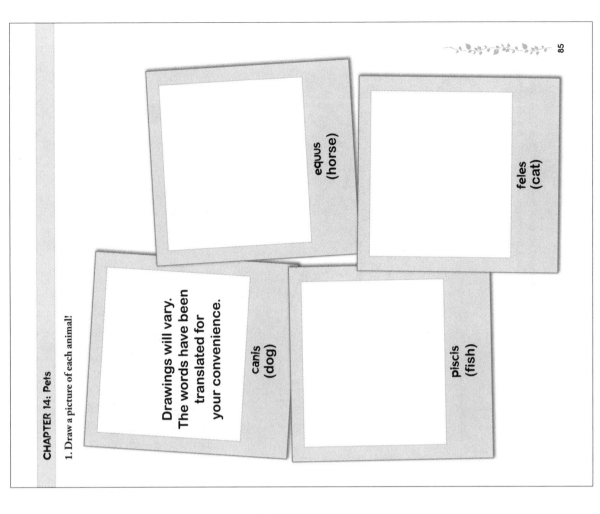

equus (horse)

feles (cat)

Drawings will vary. The words have been translated for your convenience.

canis (dog)

piscis (fish)

85

CHAPTER 13: Review

3. Translate the English into Latin by writing one Latin letter in each box.

a. Raise your hand (plural):

| A | T | T | O | L | I | T | E | ■ | M | A | N | U | S |

1

b. Open the book:

| A | P | E | R | I | ■ | L | I | B | R | U | M |

6

c. Thank you:

| T | I | B | I | ■ | G | R | A | T | I | A | S |

3

| A | G | O |

d. Open the book (plural):

| A | P | E | R | I | T | E | ■ | L | I | B | R | O | S |

2

e. Raise your hand:

| A | T | T | O | L | E | ■ | M | A | N | U | M |

5

4. Discover how well you did! In the activity above, find the numbers and write the letter in the corresponding blank below.

O   P   T   I   M   E   !
1   2   3   4   5   6

84

120 Song School Latin Activity Answers • CHAPTERS 15–16

CHAPTER 15: Animals

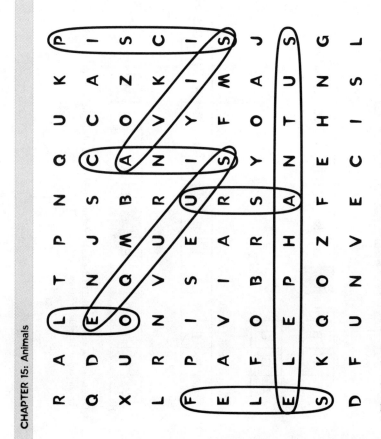

```
R  A  L  T  P  N  Q  U  K  P
Q  D  E  N  J  S  C  A  Z  I
X  U  Q  M  B  A  O  N  V  S
L  R  N  V  U  R  V  K  Y  C
F  P  I  S  E  I  A  V  I  I
E  A  V  I  A  R  R  S  Y  S
L  F  O  B  R  S  U  O  M  S
E  L  E  P  H  A  N  T  U  S
S  K  Q  O  Z  F  E  H  N  G
D  F  U  N  V  E  C  I  S  L
```

1. Translate the English words below into Latin and then find the Latin words in the word search!

a. lion   leo

b. bear   ursa

c. elephant   elephantus

d. bird   avis

Double Points if you can find: *canis, feles, equus,* and *piscis!*
Make sure you look for diagonals!

86 2. How do you say "beware of the dog" in Latin?   cave canem

CHAPTER 16: Christmas Words

1. On the scene below, draw images of all the words from this chapter. Then, label each image with its Latin word. Use the word bank to help you. The first one is done for you.

stella

Drawings will vary. The words have been translated for your convenience.

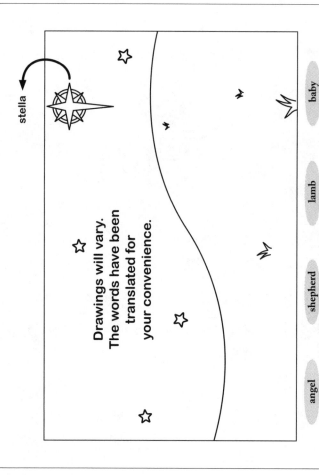

angel   angelus   shepherd   pastor   lamb   agnus   baby   infans

2. What is an infans feles? baby cat/kitten

3. How would you say "rare bird" in Latin? rara avis

87

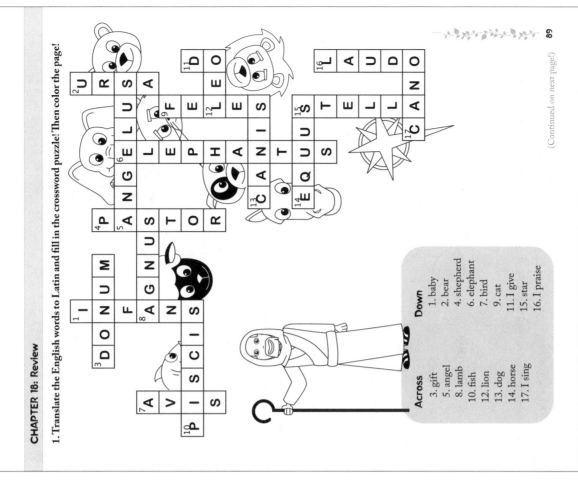

CHAPTER 18: Review

1. Translate the English words to Latin and fill in the crossword puzzle! Then color the page!

Across
3. gift
5. angel
8. lamb
10. fish
12. lion
13. dog
14. horse
17. I sing

Down
1. baby
2. bear
4. shepherd
6. elephant
7. bird
9. cat
11. I give
15. star
16. I praise

(Continued on next page!)

CHAPTER 17: More Christmas Words

1. Translate the English into Latin then match the word to the correct picture!

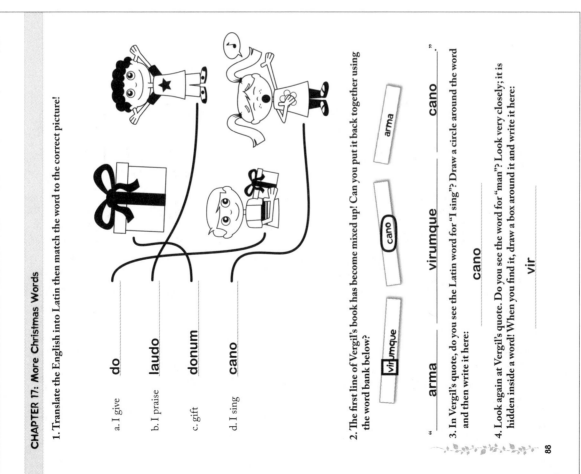

a. I give   **do**

b. I praise   **laudo**

c. gift   **donum**

d. I sing   **cano**

2. The first line of Vergil's book has become mixed up! Can you put it back together using the word bank below?

virumque   cano   arma

"__arma__ __virumque__ __cano__ ."

3. In Vergil's quote, do you see the Latin word for "I sing"? Draw a circle around the word and then write it here: __cano__

4. Look again at Vergil's quote. Do you see the word for "man"? Look very closely; it is hidden inside a word! When you find it, draw a box around it and write it here: __vir__

CHAPTER 18: Review

2. Do you remember the difference between nouns and verbs? Nouns are things you can touch and verbs are action words! Look at the words below. Circle all the nouns, and underline all the verbs.

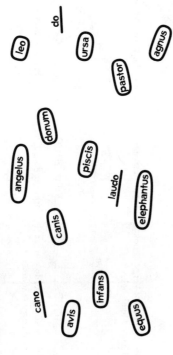

(leo)   do

(angelus)   (donum)   (ursa)

(canis)   (piscis)   (pastor)   (agnus)

(avis)   (infans)   laudo   (elephantus)

(equus)   cano

3. What is the special ending on the end of these verbs that means "I"? **O**

4. Most of the words you've learned thus far are (circle one):   (nouns)   verbs

5. Answer the questions by drawing a line to the correct word:

a. What do you see in the night sky?   do
b. What animal makes nests in trees?   canis
c. What were you when you were born?   stella
d. What animals says "woof, woof!"   feles
e. What do you do with a *donum*?   avis
f. From what animal do we get wool?   cano
g. Who takes care of flocks?   infans
h. What do you do with a song?   agnus
i. What animal says "meow!"   pastor

CHAPTER 19: The Body

1. Translate the English word into Latin. Then draw a line to the correct part of the monkey!

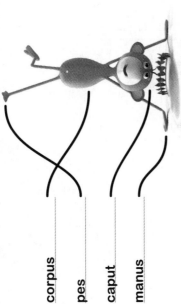

a. Body   **corpus**

b. Foot   **pes**

c. Head   **caput**

d. Hand   **manus**

2. How do you say "the voice of the people" in Latin?   vox populi

3. Many English words come from Latin words! Look at the list of English words on the left and try to match them up with the correct Latin words on the right. Here's a hint: if the words look similar, they are probably related!

a. Manuscript (*something written by hand*)   Corpus
b. Pedestrian (*someone who is on foot*)   Manus
c. Captain (*the head person in charge of a boat*)   Liber
d. Library (*a place that has lots of books*)   Pes
e. Corps (*the body of the military; the officers*)   Audi
f. Audience (*a group of people who listen*)   Caput
g. Donation (*a gift*)   Infans
h. Constellation (*a grouping of stars*)   Donum
i. Infant (*a small baby*)   Feles
j. Feline (*belonging to the cat family*)   Stella

CHAPTER 20: The Face

Using the picture and instructions below, help us create Sammy the Spy! Check off the boxes after you do each step.

- ☐ 1. Draw two **auris** on his **caput**.
- ☐ 2. Draw sunglasses over his **oculus**.
- ☐ 3. Draw a straight line for his **os**.
- ☐ 4. Draw big boots on his two **pes**.
- ☐ 5. Draw a long coat over his **corpus**.
- ☐ 6. Draw a walking stick in his **manus**.
- ☐ 7. Draw a **nares** on his face.
- ☐ 8. Draw a **stylus** behind one **auris**.
- ☐ 9. Draw a cowboy hat on his **caput**.
- ☐ 10. Draw an **avis** on one **manus**.

Drawings will vary. The sentences have been translated for you below.

1. Draw two *ears* on his head.
2. Draw sunglasses over his eyes.
3. Draw a straight line for his mouth.
4. Draw big boots on his two feet.
5. Draw a long coat over his body.
6. Draw a walking stick in his hand.
7. Draw a nose on his face.
8. Draw a pencil behind one ear.
9. Draw a cowboy hat on his head.
10. Draw a bird on one hand.

CHAPTER 21: Food Words

A	E	R	P	Y	A	Q	U	A	S
D	X	F	T	S	I	F	D	M	G
L	C	D	X	A	L	J	T	O	H
J	S	I	Z	I	E	D	V	K	N
I	Y	Q	B	O	M	P	I	N	S
S	D	R	I	U	D	V	U	Q	R
A	F	U	B	T	S	Y	A	D	D
I	E	D	G	P	O	E	S	F	
P	T	S	F	E	S	Z	N	R	L
H	U	Q	Y	J	I	X	A	K	N

1. Translate the English words below into Latin and then find the Latin words in the word search!

a. food   <u>cibus</u>

b. dinner   <u>cena</u>

c. I eat   <u>edo</u>

d. water   <u>aqua</u>

e. I drink   <u>bibo</u>

2. How many of the above words are verbs? <u>two</u>

CHAPTER 22: More Food Words

Translate the following Latin words, then draw the objects in the refrigerator!

☐ 1. A box of crustulum **cookies**
☐ 2. A loaf of panis **bread**
☐ 3. A gallon of lac **milk**
☐ 4. Pullus nuggets **chicken**
☐ 5. A basket of fructus **fruit**
☐ 6. A bottle of aqua **water**

Drawings will vary.

CHAPTER 23: Review

1. Translate the English words to Latin and fill in the crossword puzzle! Then color the page!

Across
3. bread
6. dinner
8. I drink
10. chicken
11. ear
13. hand
14. I eat
16. body
17. milk
18. mouth

Down
1. fruit
2. foot
4. nose
5. food
7. water
9. cookie
12. head
15. eye

(Continued on next page!)

CHAPTER 23: Review

2. What does *et cetera* mean? **and others**

3. The English word "pantry" comes from which Latin word? (circle one)

    lac   (panis)   cibus

4. The English word "aquarium" comes from which Latin word? (circle one)

    (aqua)   bibo   crustulum

5. Answer the questions by drawing a line to the correct word:

a. If you are thirsty, what do you do?

b. What part of your body do you use to think?

c. What liquid do you find in rivers?

d. Apples and oranges are both what kind of *cibus*?

e. What part of your body do you use to hear?

f. When you want to speak or eat, what do you use?

g. What liquid comes from cows?

h. What part of your body do you use to see?

i. What part of your body do you use to walk?

fructus   auris   bibo   os   pes   aqua   caput   oculus   lac

6. Color and label the images below!

bibo   edo   cibus

CHAPTER 24: Weather

Read the weather report for each day, then draw a picture of that day's weather in the correct circle. Then, label each image with its Latin word.

Monday: Heavy *imber* and dark *nimbus* all day long.
Tuesday: Strong *ventus* in the morning.
Wednesday: Many *nimbus* with slight chance of *nix*.
Thursday: Light *imber*, probably resulting in an *arcus* in the afternoon.
Friday: Sunshine and a few light, fluffy *nimbus*.

**Drawings will vary.
The sentences have
been translated
for you.**

MONDAY

Heavy *rain* and dark *clouds* all day long.

TUESDAY

Strong *wind* in the morning.

WEDNESDAY

Many *clouds* with a slight chance of *snow*.

THURSDAY

Light *rain*, probably resulting in a *rainbow* in the afternoon.

FRIDAY

Sunshine and a few light, fluffy *clouds*.

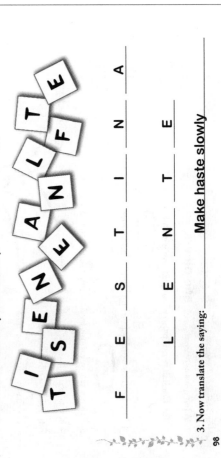

CHAPTER 25: The Seasons

1. Read the sentence about the season, then draw a line from the sentence to the season, and from the season to the weather!

summer

spring

winter

fall

a. During *hiems*, *nix* makes the ground and trees white.

b. In *autumnus*, the *ventus* blows the orange and gold leaves.

c. During *aestas* the sky is full of sun and light, fluffy *nimbus*.

d. In *ver*, *imber* falls, and you might see an *arcus*.

2. This week's Latin saying has become scrambled! Can you put the letters in the right order? Hint: make sure you work slowly!

I E N E A L F T E S T I N A

F E S T I N A

L E N T E

3. Now translate the saying: _____ **Make haste slowly**

98

CHAPTER 26: The Sky

1. Fill up the night *caelum* with lots of *stella* and then add a *luna*. On the day side, draw a big, bright *sol*.

Drawings will vary.

The translated instructions are: "Fill up the night sky with lots of *stars* and then add a *moon*. On the day side, draw a big, bright *sun*."

Night   Day

2. This week's Latin saying is *e pluribus unum*. Can you translate each part below?

e pluribus = **out of many**

unum = **one**

3. Many English words come from Latin words! Look at the list of English words on the left and try to match them up with the correct Latin words on the right. Here's a hint: if the words look similar, they are probably related!

a. Lunar *(having to do with the moon)* — Arcus

b. Arc *(a curve like that of a rainbow)* — Autumnus

c. Autumn *(another name for the fall season)* — Luna

d. Pantry *(a place where people might keep bread)* — Panis

99

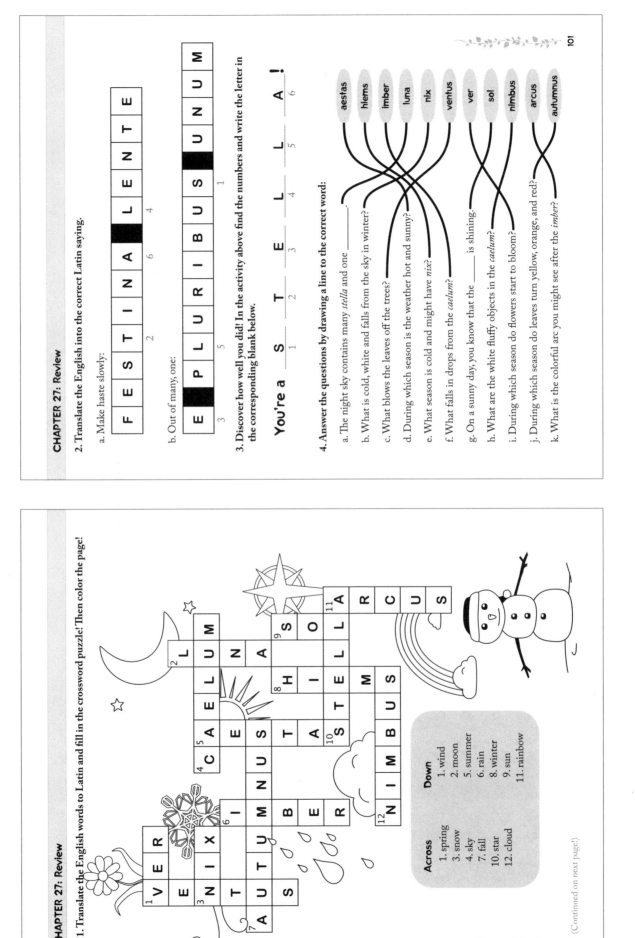

CHAPTER 27: Review

1. Translate the English words to Latin and fill in the crossword puzzle! Then color the page!

(Crossword filled in with answers)

Across
1. spring
3. snow
4. sky
7. fall
10. star
12. cloud

Down
1. wind
2. moon
5. summer
6. rain
8. winter
9. sun
11. rainbow

100 (Continued on next page!)

CHAPTER 27: Review

2. Translate the English into the correct Latin saying.

a. Make haste slowly:

F	E	S	T	I	N	A		L	E	N	T	E
	2				6			4				

b. Out of many, one:

E		P	L	U	R	I	B	U	S		U	N	U	M
3		5									1			

3. Discover how well you did! In the activity above find the numbers and write the letter in the corresponding blank below.

You're a S T E L L A !
       1 2 3 4 5 6

4. Answer the questions by drawing a line to the correct word:

a. The night sky contains many *stella* and one _____.
b. What is cold, white and falls from the sky in winter?
c. What blows the leaves off the trees?
d. During which season is the weather hot and sunny?
e. What season is cold and might have *nix*?
f. What falls in drops from the *caelum*?
g. On a sunny day, you know that the _____ is shining.
h. What are the white fluffy objects in the *caelum*?
i. During which season do flowers start to bloom?
j. During which season do leaves turn yellow, orange, and red?
k. What is the colorful arc you might see after the *imber*?

(word list: aestas, hiems, imber, luna, nix, ventus, ver, sol, nimbus, arcus, autumnus)

101

Song School Latin Activity Answers • CHAPTER 27

127

CHAPTER 28: Water Words

A	S	C	F	N	A	V	I	S	M
R	O	U	E	K	L	N	C	T	I
G	L	U	N	A	D	J	P	E	U
M	E	B	X	D	J	F	L	M	A	L	B
Q	T	G	I	A	Y	C	H	X
D	L	A	N	O	H	R	A	T
I	H	E	F	L	U	M	E	N	G
J	R	L	O	B	J	Z	U	M
A	V	U	F	P	I	S	C	I	S
Z	C	M	N	H	E	L	X	D	Y

Translate the English words below into Latin and then find the Latin words in the word search!

a. lake	lacus
b. river	flumen
c. ship/boat	navis
d. sea	mare
e. wave	unda

Double Points if you can find: *caelum, luna, stella, sol,* and *piscis!*

Make sure you look for diagonals!

CHAPTER 29: Gardening

Time to draw!

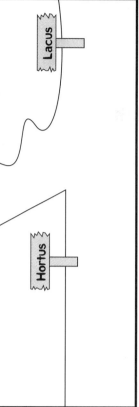

1. Draw some bumpy *ground/dirt* in the *garden.*
2. Draw a few rows of *plants* in the *garden.*
3. Put a few *flowers* on some of the *plants.*
4. In the *sky,* draw a strong *wind* blowing around three *leaves.*
5. Put a few *waves* in the *lake.*
6. On one of the *waves,* draw a small *ship/boat.*
7. Above another *wave,* draw a jumping *fish.*
8. Put a white, fluffy *cloud* in the *sky.*
9. Draw the *sun* peeking out behind the *cloud.*
10. Draw a colorful *chicken* scratching the ground in front of the *garden.*

Drawings will vary. The sentences have been translated above.

Follow the instructions and fill in the picture!
1. Draw some bumpy *humus* in the *hortus.*
2. Draw a few rows of *herba* in the *hortus.*
3. Put a few *flos* on some of the *herba.*
4. In the *caelum,* draw a strong *ventus* blowing around three *folium.*
5. Put a few *unda* in the *lacus.*
6. On one of the *unda,* draw a small *navis.*
7. Above another *unda,* draw a jumping *piscis.*
8. Put a white, fluffy *nimbus* in the *caelum.*
9. Draw the *sol* peeking out behind the *nimbus.*
10. Draw a colorful *pullus* scratching the ground in front of the *hortus.*

CHAPTER 31: Review

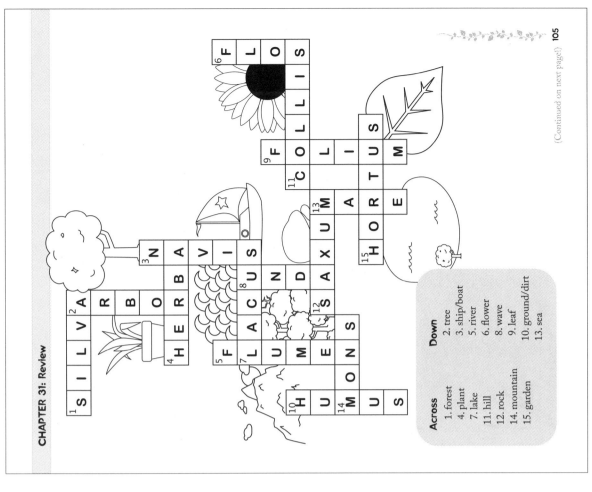

										⁶F			
										L			
										O			
¹S	I	L	²V	A						⁹F	C	O	L	L	I	S
			R								L		
			B					¹¹C	O	L	L	I	S
			O		³N						I		
	⁴H	E	R	B	A	V					U		
						I		¹³M			S		
	⁵F	L	A	C	⁸U	S	A	X	U	M			
					N		A						
					D		¹⁵H	O	R	T	U	S	
					A		E						
¹⁰H			⁷M	O	N	S							
U													
¹⁴M	O	N	S										
U													
S													

Across
1. forest
4. plant
7. lake
11. hill
12. rock
14. mountain
15. garden

Down
2. tree
3. ship/boat
5. river
6. flower
8. wave
9. leaf
10. ground/dirt
13. sea

(Continued on next page!)

CHAPTER 30: Playing Outdoors

Label each picture with its Latin name!

mons
(*mountain*)

silva
(*forest*)

arbor
(*tree*)

saxum
(*rock*)

collis
(*hill*)

CHAPTER 31: Review

2. The Latin phrases got scrambled! Help unscramble the phrases by answering the questions using the scrambled letters as a word bank.

a. If you spill *aqua* on your *feles*, how would you tell her it's your fault in Latin?

M E A   C U L P A !

b. If a *puer* has recently been on a boat, how would he say he's glad to back on "solid ground"?

T E R R A

F I R M A

3. Many English words come from Latin words! Look at the list of English words on the left and try to match them up with the correct Latin words on the right. Here's a hint: if the words look similar, they are probably related!

a. Navy (*a part of the military with many ships*)

b. Herb (*a type of plant*)

c. Foliage (*the leaves of a plant*)

d. Humble (*to be lowly, as if on the ground*)

e. Undulation (*the motion of the waves*)

f. Sylvan (*a wooded area, like a forest*)

g. Horticulture (*the science of growing a garden*)

h. Submarine (*a machine that travels under the sea*)

Herba
Unda
Navis
Humus
Mare
Silva
Folium
Hortus

END-OF-BOOK REVIEW

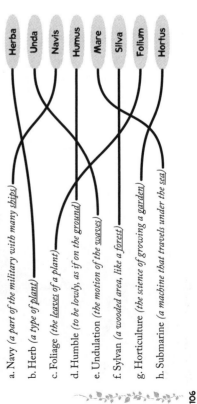

1. Label the numbered objects by writing their Latin name in the corresponding blank below. Then color the picture!

1. sol	6. silva	11. piscis
2. mons	7. puer	12. flos
3. nimbus	8. ursa	13. flumen
4. imber	9. folium	14. unda
5. arbor	10. saxum	15. herba

(Continued on next page!)

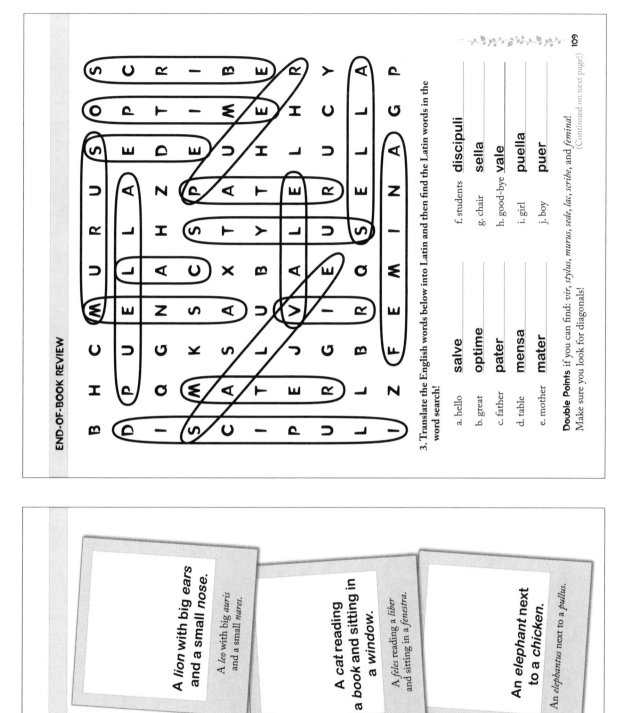

END-OF-BOOK REVIEW

3. Translate the English words below into Latin and then find the Latin words in the word search!

a. hello	**salve**	f. students	**discipuli**
b. great	**optime**	g. chair	**sella**
c. father	**pater**	h. good-bye	**vale**
d. table	**mensa**	i. girl	**puella**
e. mother	**mater**	j. boy	**puer**

Double Points if you can find: *vir, stylus, murus, sede, lac, scribe,* and *femina!* Make sure you look for diagonals!

(Continued on next page!)

109

END-OF-BOOK REVIEW

2. Draw a picture to match each of the sentences.

Drawings will vary. The sentences have been translated for you.

A horse jumping over the moon.

An *equus* jumping over the *luna.*

A lion with big ears and a small nose.

A *leo* with big *auris* and a small *nares.*

A shepherd and a lamb, sitting under a rainbow.

A *pastor* and an *agnus*, sitting under an *arcus.*

A cat reading a book and sitting in a window.

A *feles* reading a *liber* and sitting in a *fenestra.*

A dog sitting on a chair.

A *canis* sitting on a *sella.*

An elephant next to a chicken.

An *elephantus* next to a *pullus.*

(Continued on next page!)

108

END-OF-BOOK REVIEW

4. Match the Latin word to the correct picture, then color the picture!

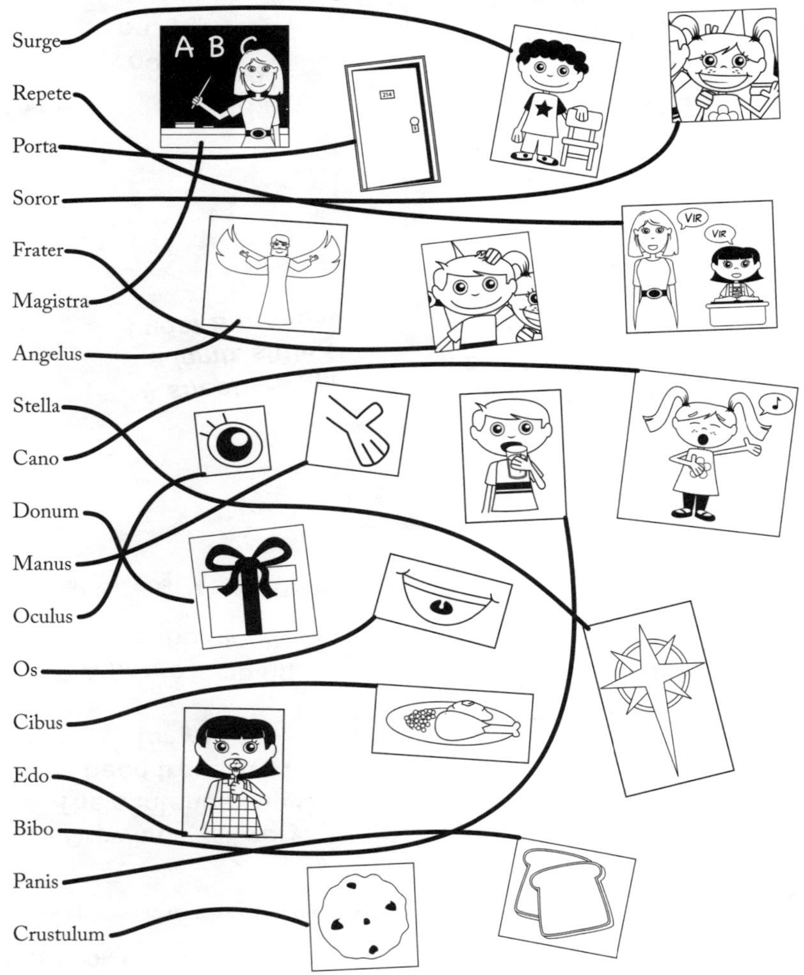
Surge
Repete
Porta
Soror
Frater
Magistra
Angelus
Stella
Cano
Donum
Manus
Oculus
Os
Cibus
Edo
Bibo
Panis
Crustulum
A B C
214
VIR
VIR

Song School Latin Book 1 Song Lyrics

Chapter 1

Salve/Vale Song [Track 1(C)/31(E)]
Here comes **magistra**,
Salve, **salve**!
Teach the **discipuli**!
Students, students!
Away goes **magistra**,
Vale, **vale**!
Good-bye, **discipuli**!
Good-bye, students!

Latin Alphabet Song [Track 2(C)/32(E)]
A B C D E F G (clap), H I J* K L M N O P (clap),
Q R S T U and V (clap), X Y Z (clap-clap).

*The J is not in the alphabet used with the classical pronunciation, but is in the alphabet used with the ecclesiastical pronunciation.

Vale Song [Track 3(C)/33(E)]
Vale! **Vale**!
Time to go, time to go, **vale**.
It's the end of the day,
And time to say,
Vale, **vale**, time to go.

Chapter 2

Nomen Song [Track 4(C)/34(E)]
Quid est tuum praenomen?
Quid est tuum praenomen?
Quid est tuum praenomen?
Tell me what your name is.
Meum praenomen est,
Meum praenomen est,
Meum praenomen est,
My name is _____.

Latin Vowels Song [Track 5(C)/35(E)]
A says **ah** and sometimes **uh**.
E says **ay** and sometimes **eh**.
I says **ee** and also **ih**.
O says **oh** and sometimes **ah**.
U says **oo** and also **uh**.
This is our Latin vowel song.

Chapter 3

Quid Agis Chant [Track 6(C)/36(E)]

Hey, HEY! **Quid agis**?
Tell me how you are, friend.
Sum, sum! Sum bene!
I am doing fine, fine!

Hey, HEY! **Quid agis**?
Tell me how you are, friend.
Sum, sum! Optime!
I am doing great, great!

Hey, HEY! **Quid agis**?
Tell me how you are, friend.
Sum, sum! Pessime!
I am doing terrible!

> **Teacher's Notes**
>
> *Optional: Clap on the second and fourth beat.
>
> Split students into two groups and have them alternate the questions/responses.

Chapter 5

Family Song [Track 8(C)/38(E)]
My **pater** is really my father,
My **mater** is really my mom.
*My **frater** is my little brother,
And I am the **soror**, you see.
Pater, pater. Pater is really my father.
Mater, mater. Mater is really my mom.
(Repeat first verse.)
Frater, frater. Frater is my little brother.
I am the **soror**, and this is my family.
(*Repeat with: "My **soror** is my little sister, And I am the **frater**, you see.")

Chapter 6

Salve Song [Track 9(C)/39(E)]
When boys get up in the morning,
You say "**Salve, puer!**"
When girls get up in the morning,
Say "**Salve, puella!**"
(clap, clap)
Each boy grows into a man,
And then he is a **vir**.
Each girl grows into a woman,
She is a **femina**.
(clap, clap)

Chapter 7

<u>Silly Sally Chant</u> [Track 10(C)/40(E)]
Silly Sally sat in her **sella**,
Eating her curds and whey,
Along came Miss Molly and sat on the **mensa**,
But her **mater** chased her away.
Serious Sam picked up a **stylus**,
And started to write in a book,
Till Luke came along and looked at that **liber**,
And said "That's MY book you took!"

> **Teacher's Notes**
>
> For the chant, have the children clap to the beat!

Chapter 8

<u>Build a Casa</u> [Track 11(C)/41(E)]
Build a **casa**, build a **casa**,
Make it nice and tall.
Don't forget to paint the **murus**,
Paint the pretty wall.
Make a window, a **fenestra**,
Let in all the light.
And make a door, a great big **porta**,
Shut it tight at night.

Chapter 10

<u>Classroom Commands Song</u> [Track 12(C)/42(E)]
Sede, sedete in your seat,
In your seat, in your seat.
Surge, surgite on your feet,
Stand up on your feet.
Scribe, scribite write so neat,
Write so neat, write so neat.
Repete, repitite,
After me repeat.

> **Teacher's Notes**
>
> Use actions or hand motions when practicing the vocabulary and singing the song.

Chapter 11

<u>Classroom Commands Song (Continued)</u>
[Track 13(C)/43(E)]
Tace, tacete - quiet please,
Quiet please, quiet please.
Audi, audite listen up,
Listen up to me.
Aperi librum – open the book,

> **Teacher's Notes**
>
> *Note that in this case "manum" and "manus" are actually the accusative forms of "manus, -us," a fourth declension noun. This should not be confused with "manus" as shown in chapter 19.

135

Open the book, open the book.
Attole manum – raise your hand,
Raise it nice and high.

Chapter 12

<u>Manners Song</u> [Track 14(C)/44(E)]
When you ask for anything you have to say **amabo te**,
When you ask for anything you have to say **amabo te**.
If you really want to have it, don't just take it away,
Just say **amabo te**.
Tibi gratias ago means thank you very much,
Tibi gratias ago means thank you, thank you very much.
If your mom gives you a cookie, say before you eat it up,
Say **tibi gratias ago**.
Please excuse me is **ignosce mihi**, please excu-use me,
Please excuse me is **ignosce mihi**, please excu-use me.
If you bump into a little man and make him spill his tea,
Say **ignosce mihi**!

Chapter 14

<u>Animal Song</u> [Track 15(C)/45(E)]
Listen to the **canis** early in the morning,
Barking at the **feles** and makin' her run away.
"Meow" said the **feles** and went to catch a **piscis**,
And she climbed on an **equus** munching on his hay.
Neigh, neigh! Meow, meow! Off we go!

Chapter 15

<u>Animal Song (Continued)</u> [Track 16(C)/46(E)]
See the little **avis** flying 'round the **leo**,
"Roar" says the **leo** and scares away the bird.
Along comes the **ursa** and eats up all the honey,
Elephantus stomps around his little elephant herd.
Tweet, tweet! Roar, roar! Off we go!

Teacher's Notes

*Practice this song as a continuation of the chapter 14 song. You might let individual students or rows of students take one line in turn—have one row or student be the bird, one the lion, etc. Encourage motions as you sing and practice the words. Each of the animals should have a representative motion or hand sign.

Chapter 16

<u>Christmas Chant</u> [Track 17(C)/47(E)]
Angelus – angel,
Stella – star,
Both appeared in the sky afar.
Pastor – shepherd,
Agnus – lamb,
Shepherds watching the little lambs.
Infans – baby,
Born in the hay,
Jesus, born on Christmas day.

Chapter 17

<u>Christmas Chant (Continued)</u> [Track 18(C)/48(E)]
Cano – I sing,
On Christmas day,
Do a donum – in a cheerful way.

Donum – present,
Do – I give,
Laudo – every day I live.

Chapter 19

<u>Action Song</u> [Track 19(C)/49(E)]

If you're happy and you know it, wave your hand – **man-us**!
If you're happy and you know it, wave your hand – **man-us**!
If you're happy and you know it, then your face will surely show it,
If you're happy and you know it, wave your hand – **man-us**!

If you're happy and you know it, stomp your foot – **pes, pes**!
If you're happy and you know it, stomp your foot – **pes, pes**!
If you're happy and you know it, then your face will surely show it,
If you're happy and you know it, stomp your foot – **pes, pes**!

If you're happy and you know it, nod your head – **ca-put**!
If you're happy and you know it, nod your head – **ca-put**!
If you're happy and you know it, then your face will surely show it,
If you're happy and you know it, nod your head – **ca-put**!

If you're happy and you know it, spin around – **cor-pus**!
If you're happy and you know it, spin around – **cor-pus**!
If you're happy and you know it, then your face will surely show it,
If you're happy and you know it, spin around – **cor-pus**!

Chapter 20

<u>Action Song (Continued)</u> [Track 20(C)/50(E)]
If you're happy and you know it, touch your nose – **na-res**!
If you're happy and you know it, touch your nose – **na-res**!
If you're happy and you know it, then your face will surely show it,
If you're happy and you know it, touch your nose – **na-res**!

If you're happy and you know it, tug your ear – **au-ris**!
If you're happy and you know it, tug your ear – **au-ris**!
If you're happy and you know it, then your face will surely show it,
If you're happy and you know it, tug your ear – **au-ris**!

If you're happy and you know it, wink your eye – **oculus**!
If you're happy and you know it, wink your eye – **oculus**!
If you're happy and you know it, then your face will surely show it,
If you're happy and you know it, wink your eye – **oculus**!

If you're happy and you know it, close your mouth – **os, os**! (finger to lips)
If you're happy and you know it, close your mouth – **os, os**!
If you're happy and you know it, then your face will surely show it,
If you're happy and you know it, close your mouth – **os, os**!

Chapter 21

<u>Edo Song</u> [Track 21(C)/51(E)]
Edo my **cibus** when it's time to eat!
Edo my **cibus** when it's time to eat!
Because I love the good food my mother makes! **Cibus**! **Cibus**!

Bibo my **aqua** when I play hard!
Bibo my **aqua** when I play hard!
When I'm thirsty, **bibo** right away! **Bibo**! **Bibo**!

It's time for **cena**, gather everyone!
It's time for **cena**, gather everyone!
We're ready to eat our **cena** tonight! **Cena**! **Cena**!

Chapter 22

<u>Cibus Chant</u> [Track 22(C)/52(E)]
Panis—bread. (clap-clap-clap)
Panis—bread. (clap-clap-clap)

Fructus—fruit. (stomp-stomp-stomp)
Fructus—fruit. (stomp-stomp-stomp)

Lac—milk. (clap-clap-clap)
Lac—milk. (clap-clap-clap)

Crustulum—cookie. (stomp-stomp-stomp)
Crustulum—cookie. (stomp-stomp-stomp)

Pullus—chicken. (clap-clap)
Pullus—chicken. (clap-clap)

Chapter 24

<u>Weather Song</u> [Track 24(C)/54(E)]
In the springtime,
When the rain comes,
Use your umbrella in the **imber**.
When the **ventus** blows,
And it's nipping at your nose,
Come inside out of the weather.

After rainstorms,
After **imber**,
Sometimes you see a pretty rainbow.
If you look up high,
There's an **arcus** in the sky,
The whole earth is glowing with a rainbow.

In the winter,
When the snow comes,
Nix covers everything in sight.
And the clouds are gray,
Every **nimbus** comes to play,
A **nix-nimbus** makes the world white.

Chapter 25

<u>Seasons Song</u> [Track 25(C)/55(E)]
A gust of fall wind, blowing leaves,
Tells me that **autumnus** is here.
The white **nix** covers each blade of grass,
And I know that the **hiems** is drawing near.

The spring flowers bloom and grass turns green,
I see that the **ver** is on its way.
The sun beats down on the summer fields,
For the **aestas** has come with a sunny day.

Chapter 26

<u>Caelum Song</u> [Track 26(C)/56(E)]
Luna moon and **stella** star,
How I wonder what you are.
Up above in the **caelum** high,
Like a diamond in the sky.
When the nighttime turns to day,
Then the **sol** comes out to stay.

Chapter 28

<u>Row Your Navis</u> [Track 27(C)/57(E)]
Navis, navis – boat,
Mare, mare – sea.
Ride the **unda**, ride the wave,
Happy as can be.

Lacus, lacus – lake,
Flumen – river, stream.
Row your **navis**, row your boat,
Life is but a dream.

Chapter 29

<u>Hortus Song</u> [Track 28(C)/58(E)]
Grab your shovel,
Put your gloves on,
It's time to plant our summer **hortus**.
Here's a **herba**, plant,
With a **folium**, a leaf,
Let's plant it in our summer **hortus**.

Plant a flower,
Plant a **flos**.
Plant pretty flowers in our **hortus**,
Plant the roots deep down.
In the **humus**, in the ground,
We love to grow a summer **hortus**.

Chapter 30

<u>Hiking Song</u> [Track 29(C)/59(E)]
Climb the mountain, climb the mountain,
Mountain – **mons**! Mountain – **mons**!
Throw a **saxum**, throw a **saxum**,
Saxum – rock! **Saxum** – rock!

Climb the **arbor**, climb the **arbor**,
Arbor – tree! **Arbor** – tree!
Roll down the **collis**, right into the **silva**,
Collis – hill! **Silva** – woods!

Classical Subjects...

SONGSCHOOL LATIN Book 2

...Creatively Taught

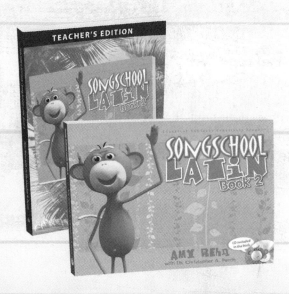

Continue the song!

Song School Latin Book 2 completes the engaging introduction to Latin started in *Song School Latin Book 1*. Weekly lessons include songs, chants, new and review vocabulary, a light introduction to Latin grammar, and derivatives, all without leaving behind the fun illustrations, stories, games, and activities! *Song School Latin Book 2* will continue to foster students' love of learning Latin while also preparing them for their journey on to *Latin for Children Primer A*.

"A six-year-old boy's favorite part of school is Latin? Want to know why? We're using Song School Latin. We love this curriculum. I cannot recommend this book enough for the family who wants to gently introduce their early elementary student to Latin."

—Amy, *Heart of the Matter Online*

Includes

Video

Audio

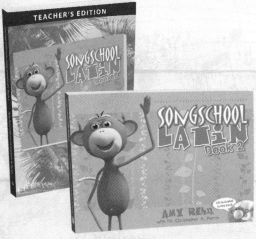

Full Program Includes:
- *Song School Latin Book 2 Student Edition*
- *Song School Latin Book 2 Teacher's Edition*
- *Song School Latin Book 2 Streaming Video (or 3-DVD Set)*
- *Latin Monkey Match 2 Flashcard Game*

Free sample songs and chapters at www.ClassicalAcademicPress.com

Your Latin Journey

Lower Grammar

You Can **Start** *Here* ↴

Grades 1–2

Grades 2–3

Upper Grammar

Start or Continue **Here** ↴

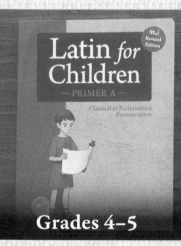

Grades 4–5

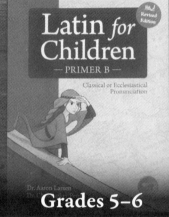

Grades 5–6

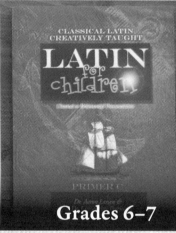

Grades 6–7

Ready for **National Latin Exam Prep**

Middle & High School

or **Here** ↴

Grades 7–8+

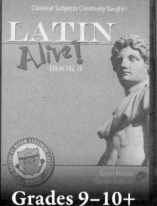

Grades 8–9+

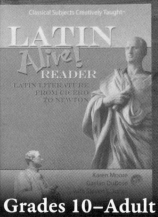

Grades 9–10+

Grades 10–Adult

Ready for

| National Latin Exam Level I | National Latin Exam Level II | National Latin Exam Level III or IV Prose | National Latin Exam Level III or IV Prose |

Classical Subjects...

Writing & Rhetoric

...Creatively Taught

The Writing & Rhetoric series (W&R) prepares students in the art of writing well and speaking persuasively. Students will learn the skills of the *progymnasmata*, a classical writing system so dynamic, so effective, that it outlasted the Roman Empire, the Middle Ages, and the Renaissance, and has even survived into early modern times. Students will enjoy the journey to mastering modern composition—including narrative, expository, descriptive, and persuasive writing—while simultaneously developing unique rhetorical muscle.

"My [students] love this. The stories are wonderful and engaging, and we have had so much fun. They are making great progress and have moved from dreading their writing assignments to eagerly anticipating them each week."
—Teren, Cottage School director

"This is a very well-thought-out, creatively constructed, effective writing program. Not only did I see my kids really thinking and improving their writing skills, they actually enjoyed it along the way!" —Cassandra, owner/writer at *The Unplugged Family*

Includes
Audio

Full Program Includes:
• W&R Student's Edition
• W&R Teacher's Edition, featuring:
  • the complete student text
  • answer keys
  • teacher's notes and explanations
  • descriptions and examples of excellent student writing for every writing assignment
• W&R Audio Files, featuring the readings from the student edition

www.ClassicalAcademicPress.com